THE SAGA OF
NICHOLAS STONER

A TALE OF THE
ADIRONDACKS

THE SAGA OF
NICHOLAS STONER

A TALE OF THE
ADIRONDACKS

DONALD R. WILLIAMS

NORTH COUNTRY BOOKS
Utica, New York

A Tale of the
ADIRONDACKS

Copyright © 1972
by
Donald R. Williams

First Printing 1972
Willard Press, Boonville, N.Y.

All Rights Reserved

First paperback printing 2004
North Country Books

ISBN 0-925168-88-2

Williams, Donald R. (Donald Ross), 1934-
  The saga of Nicholas Stoner, or, A tale of the Adirondacks / Donald R. Williams.
      p. cm.
  Originally published: Wells, N.Y. : Adirondack Books, c1969.
  ISBN 0-925168-88-2 (alk. paper)
  1. Stoner, Nicholas, b. 1762. 2. Pioneers--New York (State)--Adirondack
Mountains--Biography. 3. Trappers--New York (State)--Adirondack Mountains--
Biography. 4. Frontier and pioneer life--New York (State)--Adirondack Mountains.
5. Outdoor life--New York (State)--Adirondack Mountains. 6. Adirondack
Mountains (N.Y.)--Biography. 7. Adirondack Mountains (N.Y.)--Social life and cus-
toms--18th century. I. Title: Saga of Nicholas Stoner. II. Title: Tale of the
Adirondacks. III. Title.
  F127.A2W64 2004
  974.7'503'092--dc22

                    2004013808

NORTH COUNTRY BOOKS
Utica, New York

Dedicated to
The Lovers of the Mountains
who follow in Nick's footsteps.

ACKNOWLEDGMENTS

Writing the story of Nicholas Stoner has been made much easier and more interesting because of the tales recorded by Jeptha R. Simms who purposely recorded Stoner's life, "To place on record what can still be gathered respecting him, to live in future story." The many folk tales and documents, historical data and newspaper articles have added to the story. You may also note a dash of imagination in the tale.

Our area abounds in "history buffs" as well as history. There are several who knowingly or unknowingly assisted in recording THE SAGA OF NICHOLAS STONER. Without their help it would be an incomplete tale.

THE SAGA OF NICHOLAS STONER would still be my summer pastime if it were not for the patience of my wife and the persistence of my secretary. A sincere thank you to Beverly and Barbara.

D. Williams

TABLE OF CONTENTS

Part I — The Great Wilderness

Part II — Nicholas Stoner — The Boy

Part III — Nicholas Stoner — The Patriot

Part IV — Nicholas Stoner — The Man

Part V — Nicholas Stoner — Trapper and Hunter

Part VI — Nicholas Stoner — Another War

Part VII — Nicholas Stoner — A Long Life

PREFACE

It has not been proven that there is a bond between man and the earth from which he sprang, but there are indications of some unseen attraction, some unseen connection between man and the out-of-doors. The value and effect of a wilderness experience on a man's life is unreportable, yet enough evidence exists to make it worthy of attention.

Such is THE SAGA OF NICHOLAS STONER, a man of the land whose whole life was centered about the great out-of-doors and the Adirondack Mountains he loved. The very land in which he lived molded and shaped his character and beliefs. He continued, throughout his life, to look to the wilderness for release from the tensions of life and for peace of mind.

The life and happiness of Nicholas Stoner should serve as a model for all of us, and his love and appreciation of a wooded glen, a cool mountain lake, a majestic sunset or a mountain-top view is a lesson for many who have lost the ability to relax in today's fast-moving world.

Read THE SAGA OF NICHOLAS STONER and venture forth into the great out-of-doors for your own wilderness experience as you work hard at the business of living.

Donald R. Williams

PART I

THE GREAT
WILDERNESS

Chapter I

The Great Wilderness

The earth was covered with the stillness — the kind of stillness known only to those who have penetrated the depths — the depths of the Great Wilderness. The Great Wilderness where the stillness was interrupted by a strange and new sound — a cracking and crunching — a cracking and crunching marking the birth of those rolling hills, upheavals in the earth's surface, long before life as we know it existed.

The primeval sea rippled and bubbled as small deposits trickled down from the mainland into the submerged continental shelf, marking the birth of the great mountains over one billion years ago. The next five hundred million years were marked by vast unknown compressive forces erupting to work on the sedimentary particles. Yes, the precambrian stillness was broken by the buckling and thrusting upward to the sky of the most magnificent and majestic mountains ever created on our earth. These ancestral mountains were then to be eroded and flattened, until they were once again beneath the westward advancing eastern sea, never to be seen by man. Additional, brief, but gentle upwarp and erosion, faulting and eventual uploading of eastern North America with new and vigorous erosion created the mountains that today are known to all as the Adirondacks.

Then came the ice — ripping, gouging and plowing — removing the deep residual soils and laying bare the bedrock to be scoured and polished by the moving rock debris embedded in the ice. High and low places were

marked by glaciation. V-sloped valleys were remodeled
to U-sloped configurations. Scars, still to be seen today,
were left on the exposures of bedrock.

And when the damage was complete the melting began, and the ice retreated, leaving behind dams of rock
rubble and the beginnings of many beautiful lakes
and valleys. Vegetation reclaimed the lands as they rebounded above the seas, and our present day densely
forested mountains — The Adirondacks — were free to
grow to maturity.

The naked trees of winter standing stark and alone
in the whiteness, the buds and birds of spring creating
an abundance of activity, the many hues of summer
green mixing with the deep woods moss, the long shadows of the autumn sun highlighting the colors of the
leaves, the crimson and darkened reds, the true yellow
and the many shades of gold and browns, adding majesty
and beauty, and the frost-touched foliage balancing with
the darker colors of her evergreens covering the hillsides,
lure her sons to penetrate her depths, to seek her game,
to enjoy her beauty, and to search for peace, the peace
found only when those ingredients of *beauty,* beauty of a
foaming-white mountain stream, the beauty of a leafy
hillside, the beauty of a cool mountain lake; *of stillness,*
the stillness of the deep woods where all sounds are
distant and unknown, the stillness where the animals are
unafraid of man's intrusion; *of companionship* of man
or beast, the companionship of closeness, Adirondack
imbued; *of fresh air* found only when man leaves "civilization" — are balanced and mixed and aged until they
produce a world, another world, needed and sought by
man today and yesterday.

And this is the story of those mountainous hills told
because man has lived and because one man, a true son

of the Adirondacks, has made his mark on time, on the minds of other men and on the mountains that he loved.

Yesterday — a son — a true son of the Adirondacks walked her virgin woods and upheaved hills — searching for the Truth and a way of life — gaining the fierce, sometimes antagonistic, independence characteristic of and so familiar to survival in the Adirondacks. To many, he was a war hero; to others, he was a good man to have in the community; to some, he was a "lazy trapper"; to himself, he was one who believed in fair play — in doing the best that he knew and in constant turmoil of mind in search of happiness.

His Indian-like appreciation of the wilderness, his early entrance into manhood, his self-experienced appreciation of war, his belief in the Creator of all, his love and respect for women, and his everyday dealings with the early inhabitants of the Adirondacks and Mohawk Valley combined to create a man, more than ordinary, who lives today in the minds of others — and whose name lives on in his community — Nicholas Stoner — a road, a lake, an inn, a club chapter, all reflecting in the glory of and carrying on a name so familiar to the "leatherland" Fulton County, New York State. Nick Stoner, the man to match the mountains, who gained his strength and inspiration from the mountains, who found his peace in the mountains, who lived for his life in the mountains, and who, by rekindling the memory of the man, leads us to the mountains; fulfilling a destiny of a heart wise in the ways of man and the Adirondacks.

PART II

NICHOLAS STONER
The Boy

CHAPTER II

Nick and New York

Boyhood in the city, New York City of the 18th century, proved to mold a boy who enjoyed a good prank —a boy who found excitement in the everyday world and who was possessed with wanting to be happy and making others happy—a boy who later learned a respect for a wilderness completely foreign to his early years.

Nick Stoner reluctantly left his home to study, through the generosity of his favorite uncle, John Binkus, who early saw the genius in the boy and decided that he should be in school learning to read. By that time, Nick had become accustomed to enjoying his freedom to hop a streetcar and to make a trip to the docks where he could spend hours exchanging jokes and stories with the sailors, and learning to read could easily tie an adventurous soul, such as Nick, to drudgery. Matter of fact, it was during one of these episodes that Nick acquired a small gold ring in his right ear which he wore throughout his life. It was placed in his ear by one of his favorite old sea captains who promised, "I'll bring ye the other one on the next trip if 'n ye don't cry while I'st put this'n in." Nick, fearing nothing, met the challenge and agreed to the bargain. However, his old friend was never heard from again and the sentimental Nick decided to wear the ring forever.

But, surprisingly, the generosity of Uncle John, his benefactor, opened up new horizons to Nick. He was a quick learner and was soon reading tales of adventure

and humor that he never knew existed. And with innocent boyish curiosity, triggered by his mother's religious
belief and the God-fearing belief of his dock-side friends,
he began to search the depth of the family Bible for
answers to his questions of many years, a habit easily
acquired and never forgotten. And these early adventures with books proved to be a positive influence
throughout his adventurous life.

Nick loved books and spent many hours lost in a
book, usually with a tale of the frontier. It captured his
imagination until he knew that the wilds would be the
place for him, the place for a boy too full of the excitement of life to be confined to city streets.

On several occasions, Nick mentioned his desire to
leave the city to his father, Henry Stoner, who, enjoying
a rather successful time in his "speculating business,"
closed his ears to any mention of leaving. Henry had
a family to support, and he knew it took money to buy
the things they needed and wanted. Trying to "specu-
late" on the frontier, where money is in short supply
and goods are scarce, would mark the end of his occupation. Yet, Henry was an adventurous person, and he
often thought that he would like to gamble on a move to
the frontier, leaving the pressures and risk of his business
behind him. He knew that he would enjoy a wilderness
farm if it wasn't for wanting so many worldly goods for
his family.

However, Nick's mother had watched with interest
the change in her boy, his complete engrossment with
books, his intense interest in the frontier, and his serious searching of the Bible. Her knowledge of her husband's adventurous spirit and her dissatisfaction with
his occupation, bordering as it was on sometimes taking
advantage of his fellow-man, contributed to her startling

announcement at the family dinner table on April 18, 1770, "I think the Stoner family should join the pioneers and journey to the Northern New York frontier!!"

Nick was thrilled by the trip up the Hudson on one of the many sloops he had seen in the New York harbor. The journey past the Palisades and along the Hudson Highlands was unlike anything he had ever experienced. And little did he dream that the beautiful Catskill Mountains were so close to his boyhood home. The flats around Albany and Schenectady misled young Nick into thinking that he had reached the end of the mountains, and it wasn't until the canoe journey up the Mohawk to Caughnawaga that he noticed the wild mountainous country again. The family settled on a lot provided by Sir William Johnson, a Johnstown landowner and Indian Superintendent, six miles east of Johnstown near Fonda's Bush. Mrs. Stoner felt a little reluctant about settling in such a remote spot and probably would have felt more so if she knew that it would be two years before they had any neighbors.

CHAPTER III

Nick Meets the Frontier

The thick virgin wilderness around the Stoner cabin was slowly cleared by Henry and his boys — although they were torn between their love of each tree and the need to have room to live. They had enjoyed the traditions of the frontier since their arrival including the logging-bee—excitement mixed with hard work. Men had come from miles around to help clear the land of the troublesome stumps and useless trunks of trees after cutting logs for the cabin. The work had been followed by wrestling matches and generous suppers prepared by the womenfolk — the favorite being flapjacks with maple syrup from the forest trees. Nick loved the maple syrup at first taste and soon learned how the Indians had taught the settlers to tap the mighty maples of the forest in the spring. Nick was naturally curious and endlessly questioned anyone who would supply him with information. He learned how the sap was boiled to make the rich, sweet syrup, or boiled longer to make "jackwax" and sugar. He tasted the tea made from dried peas and maple sugar.

Nick and his brothers and sisters eagerly looked forward to the annual "jackwax" party, ranking it as a highlight of the year. The tubs of fresh clean snow from the woods were lined up, and the hot, sweet syrup was poured on, to harden and to be devoured by the anxious children. Nick ate all he could until, as he usually said, "it tickles my throat!"

Nick's daily contact with the forest and her products began to build a desire in the inquisitive youth to learn more about this great wilderness in his back yard. He used each spare hour to venture into the woods beyond his father's stump fences until he felt confident and at home with the woods and the woodland creatures. It became his job to supply food for the family by bringing home the game from the forest. He soon taught himself how to walk and to move while in the forest. He taught himself how to find his way back to the cabin by the use of the sun. He even made a night hike using the North Star as his guide. He learned to eat the woodland plants and roots and wild berries and nuts and to chew spruce gum. He learned to stalk the wild creatures and observe their habits. And he even learned to estimate the temperature by adding forty to the number of chirps a cricket could make in fifteen seconds on a hot summer night. It was after this self-introduction to the ways of the forest that Nick, now a confident "half-educated" woodsman, was to receive his real initiation and gain new and immense respect for the deep and, as the maps said, uninhabitable northern woods, Couchsachrage country.

Nick headed out about 7 o'clock in the morning with his favorite pack basket on his back containing a small lunch and his poncho. The day was bright and sunny, but Nick generally thought that his poncho might come in handy for a sudden, over the mountain, thunderstorm.

Nick set a fast pace through the Sacondaga[1] Vlaie — a spot named "much water" by the Indians, a spot where Nick imagined the future location of "a great Sacondaga lake" if man decided to hold the waters back — intending to do a little fishing and exploring in the "Kunjamuk" range to the northeast of the Sacondaga trail—the woodland highway used by the Indians as a North-South

---

[1]Original spelling.

route. He set his direction with the bright sun off his right shoulder and covered the distance to the forks of the Sacondaga by nightfall. He spent the night camping along the Indian trail, where he discovered, and was thrilled by, a bed of fossils left by some ancient sea. He left the Sacondaga with the morning sun over his right shoulder, and ten pounds of fossils in his pack. By noon he had covered the thickly wooded distance from the Sacondaga to what he called the big range country because of the many animal tracks and droppings. He circled around a couple of small lakes with the afternoon sun now over his right shoulder. Nick decided it was too late in the day to fish, and he had better start back for a familiar trail home. It was quite a trip for a novice woodsman who began his life in New York City.

Nick slowly made his way down what he thought was the Kunjamuk River, walking in the water where stone and sand made it possible, enjoying the feeling of the cool mountain spring water on his tired feet, walking through the tufted swamplands claimed by the tall growing grasses and weeds, where dangerous footing made for extremely slow going, and walking through the deep woods to avoid the grass pinks and cotton grass, the pitcher plants, and the bog rosemary now claiming the swamplands of the Kunjamuk. Nick passed a surprising number of grasslands where the shoulder-high grasses and flowering plants were reclaiming the lakes of yesteryear. He startled and was startled by a number of partridges winding off into the underbrush. He stopped occasionally to drink from the pure, clear mountain stream and to splash its cooling water on his sweating brow. Nick liked nothing better than to bury his face into his hands filled with the cold waters of a mountain stream. He often closed his eyes and did it at home, pretending that he was deep in the woods by a cool mountain stream.

Suddenly, to Nick's momentary alarm, the sky began to darken as the sun indicated early evening. Nick didn't know how much farther he had to go. He felt the pangs of panic nibbling at his heart and brain and recalled stories of other men lost forever in the great wilderness. He knew that you weren't lost unless you panicked and stumbled wildly through the woods in a circle. Nick calmed himself and decided to save a little food and to sleep in the forest for the night and to strike out again in the morning, a tough decision for a young boy uninitiated to the real wilderness of the mountains! He had little to look forward to the next morning — the rough trail was discouraging. He had been following the river, because, as he had been told by those wise in the ways of the forest — "Water will take you some place."

Nick hastily used his fish line to lash a pole between two trees to make a small lean-to with his raincoat and a few fallen branches. And just in time; the clouds parted and dumped a steady stream of cool rain water on the now fast-dampening woods. Nick erased any thought of getting a fire started.

Nick spent the first part of the night, between the shivers and shakes of the coldness and nervousness of a young boy lost in the woods, doubting the wisdom of the long, tough journey so far, more than worrying over the distance ahead. He uttered a small prayer in his mind before dozing off for a restless sleep. During the night he heard the prowling of the mean and wild black bear. He could smell their wet fur in the woods as they grunted and hunted. He swung wildly and often at the noisy, buzzing, biting mosquitoes.

Never in his life had Nick felt the pangs of fear so

close to his heart and mind as the hoot of the night owl broke the stillness or the loud, yet distant, crash of a twig marked the movement of some unknown beast. And never in his life had Nick felt so close and dependent upon God as the reading of the Bible in his early years now began to assume new importance in his life—an importance that was to continue to be a real influence as the boy became a man. And never had Nick felt so far from a familiar voice and so close to the possibility of facing death before the dawn—never to emerge from the forest that until tonight had been his friend.

Nick thought of his folks at home and knew that his mother would be worried and afraid of what might have happened to him. He really was all right, he told himself, but he was helpless as far as notifying anyone that this was true. It was a new sensation to Nick, but one that in later years he learned to accept as part of his life in the outdoors. And as his mind cleared, Nick actually relaxed and felt a new enjoyment overwhelm him as the mixture of the hemlock-scented mountain air, the misty, fog-brushed damp woods, the faint sounds of the animals in the woods filled his senses with an undescribable sensation—as his spirit gained new strength and confidence from his surroundings.

Nick spied a few fleet-footed, white-tailed deer in the early morning light. A friendly porcupine looked him over and sauntered off in search of a morning morsel. The birds began to wake and loudly claim their individual territory, and the playful chipmunks began to scramble and quarrel in the branches above. Nick felt his loneliness leave as the cheerful chatter and clatter of the small creatures of the woods encouraged him to be up and away.

Shortly after dawn Nick began making his way

slowly down-river, passing many beaver dams and lodges. He then knew first-hand why this was claimed by the Mohawks for their hunting grounds and was called "COUCHSACHRAGE" or Beaver Hunting Grounds. He paused in a flooded glen to see if he could spy the couple who had chewed through the many trees, some as thick as six inches.

He found a pile of freshly peeled sticks and some long narrow chips and knelt quietly to listen. Nick felt the presence of beaver. It might have been a ripple in the water, a slight stirring within the beaver lodge or Nick's vivid imagination, but he knew the beaver were around. He reached out with a stick and loosened a portion of the well-built dam. It wasn't long before the brown furry head of a busy beaver broke the surface and scanned the surroundings for the source of trouble. Nick watched the repair work quietly until the thought of his journey stirred him to action. He had a fleeting thought that we could learn a lot from the busy beaver.

Nick's mind was clearer now than it had been the previous evening, and he began to think things through in some sort of logical fashion. Nick had learned once, from an Abenaki Indian, Sabel Benedict, who had stopped at his father's farm, that the Sacondaga trail ran many miles north to where the redskin had his home. Since he was somewhere east of the trail, a day's journey west should put him on it. So, with the morning sun behind him, he left the river and set his hiking pace through the woods. The thought of escaping from the forest that had threatened to swallow him filled Nick with new confidence and added strength to his step.

Nick's journey through the climax forests filled with tall, century-old trees renewed his spirit and stirred his deep love for the wilderness. The thick over-growth above and the soft forest floor beneath his feet were unmatched by anything Nick could imagine. His heart beat with excitement as he discovered a hillside of pink ladyslippers, a garden of woodland-green ferns, and a patch of wild blueberries. He enjoyed the many encounters with the innocent animals who appeared unafraid of his intrusion.

Nick soon covered the distance over the rolling hills, across the short steep ridges, and by mid-afternoon came to an abrupt stop as he found himself on the trail. Nick rightly assumed it was the Sacondaga trail and turning left he commenced the final leg of his journey, down along the beautiful Sacondaga — enjoying the trip as much as his Indian brothers who came before him. Thus, what could have been a trip of tragedy ended as a journey of joy for the young woodsman who forever thereafter held the greatest of respect for the wild Couchsachrage country.

CHAPTER IV

Nick at Johnson Hall

Nick enjoyed his family's cabin in the wilderness, but he also looked forward to the journey to Kalaneka, "The place where one stops to fill his bowl with food and drink," the thriving community near Johnson Hall known as Johnstown. The presence of the Indians at this junction of six trails, along with the John Jacob Astor fur trading post and, of course, Johnson Hall, contributed to Nick's excitement and enthusiasm and accounts for his volunteering to go for supplies whenever the need arose.

The July 7th sun was just breaking over the horizon when young, now eleven-year-old, Nick stirred on his straw tick and soon bounced to the floor as if he had urgent business that day. And he did. Today he was going to town and join in the fun at Johnson Hall. His father had heard from some passing Indians that a gathering of the tribes had been underway since mid-June at Johnson Hall, and well over six hundred Indians were expected. This meant serious talk for the elders but fun and games and food for the young. And Nick, always ready to accept any challenge, meant to join in the fun and show the Indians a white boy they couldn't beat. Nick had seen these sport day games at Johnson Hall on a previous trip and he knew it was rough and tumble and not for the frail of body or spirit.

Nick's mother was up and about, to make certain that Nick ate a hearty breakfast, which he did, without any coaxing, because he knew that he would need it before the day was over. She also packed him a lunch to take along "just in case he got hungry before Sir William set his tables." Nick's mother had learned that the hearty appetite of her eleven-year-old son was never satisfied. She complained noisily about the amount he consumed, but she secretly enjoyed watching him put away large slices of her homemade bread along with the more than adequate portions she put in front of him. She shared her husband's pride in their strong and healthy, full-spirited son.

Nick parted, with a quick kiss on his mother's cheek, and set a good pace for Johnstown. He moved steadily and silently through the woods, spying an occasional deer and porcupine in the soft morning light. The cool nip in the mountain air gave a briskness to Nick's gait and he covered the miles through the wilderness with vigor. His early self-training in the wilderness had taught him the value of using a good hiking pace, hour after hour. This early practice had also earned him the reputation of moving with the caution of a trapper, which became his later claim to fame, and with the stillness of a panther.

None of the settlers from Caughnawaga along the Mohawk turnpike to the outposts in Piseco were surprised when Nick appeared out of the woods with a friendly "hello."

Nick also numbered some Indians among his friends. On this particular trip, he overtook a group of Mohawks who were on their way to Johnson Hall. Nick admired their skill in the woods and, upon many occasions, copied the Mohawk ways. The Indians in later years were known to admire the woodland skills of Nick Stoner as well as to fear his wrath when they crossed him by disturbing his trap lines or invading his wilderness camps.

The group that Nick joined journeying to Johnson

Hall was excited about the coming events. They chattered happily in the Mohawk language, and Nick surmised, by his brief knowledge of their tongue, and his observations made it plain, that they liked Sir William, "Warraghiyegey" (He-who-does-much), and couldn't wait to spend some time with him as their host. They were dressed in their finest rawhide leggings and shirts and carried their brightest blankets in a roll for the chilly nights.

Nick arrived at Johnstown and hurried through the errands for his family. He hid the supplies in the nearby woods and quickly set out for Johnson Hall. He took the shortcut through Hall Street, down the hill and up past the well-kept homes of the German farmers and the Scottish Highlanders, descendants of the same family as Sir William, who had brought them over in 1773 as tenants. Nick had previously appraised them as rich, fierce, and quarrelsome, and he secretly hoped that they would stay away from the festivities.

Nick soon found two of his friends, Aaron Griswald and Jim Dunn, and they made plans for participating in the day's events. Some concern was shown over the lack of a horse for Sir William's special horse race in which the rider sits backward on the horse. However, Nick assured his friends that he would be able to borrow a horse when the time came, knowing full well that Sir William usually supplied some horses. He knew that Sir William always awarded a bearskin jacket to the day's best player, and Nick wasn't taking any chances on missing any of the events.

There was some word among the gathering crowd that the lord of the house, Sir William, was not feeling up to the day's events but would try to join the group later in the day. Nick was disappointed that Sir William, whom he admired so much, would not attend and enjoy the fun in his usual fashion. He also selfishly wished that Sir William would be present to present him with his prize, if he won, which he intended to try his best to do.

Nick's thoughts turned to the day's events as he listened to Jim and Aaron boast of their prowess in boxing and racing. Nick knew, and his friends knew, that he could out-box and out-run both of them, but as he sized up the Indian crowd, he began to wonder. The thought crossed his mind that maybe he should wait until he was older, but it was quickly dismissed by the sudden squealing and shouting as one of Sir William's men arrived on the scene with a greased pig.

The braves quickly lined up along with Nick and his friends as preparations were made to release the pig. It was a contest without rules except that the winner must carry the pig back to the point of origin. The pig was released, a gun was fired, and they were off, that is, all except Nick. He had stopped quietly to cover his chest, hands and arms with a thick coating of dirt. He surmised that he could hold onto a greased pig much easier if dirty, than if smooth and clean.

Nick quickly joined the jostling, fighting, scampering group as the squealing pig escaped first from one boy and then another. Nick watched his chance and scurried in on one of these occasions, pushed two braves aside, and dove onto the squealing, slippery pig. His gamble paid off. The dirt enabled him to get a good grip on the pig's legs as he ran for the finish line.

Suddenly the whole world crashed upon him as a large group of the surprised braves came to their senses and tackled the running boy. Nick, holding a death grip on the pig, wiggled and swung the squealing pig until he held off his attackers. In this manner, he made his way to the finish line, and the first race was his. The cheers of the crowd and his friends made Nick swell with pride and happiness. He also registered the thought that his father would be proud of him for bringing home a pig to help feed the growing Stoner family.

There was a slight delay in the day's events while the officials decided to save the greased pole, the ugliest face, and the worst song contests for later in the day in hopes that Sir William would be able to enjoy them. Nick was just noting a slight pain in his right shoulder and arm from the body contact in the first contest when the group gathered in a circle for the boxing matches.

Again, it was a contest unshackled by rules and ended when one of the boxers could not continue and/or gave up. Apparently, previous contests had left two of the Indians without opponents, and they were immediately matched against each other. This gave Nick the much-needed opportunity again to observe their style and tactics. Nick's keen mind and quick grasp of the essentials served him well in his forthcoming foray.

The bigger of the two braves ended the fight within five minutes by a sharp blow to the stomach of his opponent and a quick uppercut to his jaw. Nick made a mental note to guard his stomach as the brave began to shout in a loud voice.

Nick knew the broad-shouldered, slim-waisted Indian was challenging all comers, and a quick look at his two friends made it obvious, as a hush fell over the crowd, that Waunterio, the Indian Brave, was going to be the champion of the day.

As the officials stepped forward to declare Waunterio the winner of the boxing event, Nick swallowed hard, fought back his doubts and fears, and jumped forward shouting, "Let a true son of the woods show you how to fight."

Waunterio didn't wait for the official word but laughed at his small opponent and lunged at Nick landing a glancing blow on the right side of his head. Nick countered with a quick right which caught the unsuspecting Indian below his right rib cage and left him grunting with surprise. He couldn't believe that someone so slight of stature could land so powerful a blow. But this only served to make him a harder opponent for Nick to beat, as the Indian now knew that Nick was going to be at least an even match.

The crowd, in their enthusiasm and excitement, closed in, making a small "ring" for the two opponents. The quick exchange of blows was heard by all as each knocked the other, back and forth into the waiting arms of the crowd where they were immediately rebounded into the fight.

Nick's head was spinning and his desire for winning was weakening when his opponent, accustomed to Indian rules, landed a sharp kick to Nick's left hip, catapulting him into the dust. Now, Nick had been taught to fight fair, no matter how great the odds, and he was quick to anger when someone purposely disregarded what he considered right.

Nick slowly raised himself out of the dust, amid the laughter of the crowd, and allowed time for his head to clear and for his anger to subside. He knew that anger was an enemy, not a friend. Nick's slow maneuver gave Waunterio a chance to move in for another kick, but Nick was ready for him and grabbing his leg with both hands, he raised it high in the air and landed Waunterio on his head and shoulder at the feet of the laughing crowd. Now the tables were turned. Waunterio, in a blind rage over Nick's quick maneuver, lunged forward threatening to kill Nick with his bare hands. The nimble Nick sidestepped, allowing the lunging Indian to disappear in the crowd. As the crowd scrambled for safety, Nick followed up his advantage by landing a powerful right swing on the jaw of his opponent as he raised his head to look for Nick. Nick followed, fully intending to press his advantage, but quickly noted that Waunterio had had enough and was trying to disappear in the crowd. Nick, however, called him back for a friendly handshake and amid the cheers of the crowd they agreed to fight again when Sir William had his field days.

Nick was treated to a cold bucket of water and a drink by his admiring friends and, feeling the results of the first two contests, decided to sit the sack race out. He had really already decided in his elation over his success that it was a "kids'" race but said nothing, knowing that Jim and Aaron had looked forward to it.

As the contestants lined up, Nick noted that some of the Scottish Highlander boys had joined the group. He made a mental note that trouble would result, and it wasn't long before the officials were quarreling with a group at the finish of the sack race. Apparently, Aaron had beaten their champion by one jump, and they wanted a rematch. Nick moved in quietly and told the leader of the group that Aaron was the winner and "that was that." The issue then settled itself as the officials began to line up the horses for the backwards ride.

Nick knew that this was Sir William's special race, and he hoped that the great man would attend to see it. And sure enough, a glance toward the manor house revealed Sir William leading three of his finest horses toward the starting line. Nick and his two friends, along with a half dozen Indians, sprang forward to beg their use for the contest. Sir William was not only a lover of fun, but was a wise man. He immediately released the horses and with a hearty laugh, shouted, "He who catches them, can ride them."

Friends of the family always mentioned that Nick had an intelligent brow, and his actions in a crisis seemed to bear this out. Instead of dashing headlong after the horses along with the Indians and his friends, Nick quickly trotted off for Sir William's horse barn. His gamble paid off as the horses circled around and headed for the stable. Nick quickly grabbed two of them before they crossed the Hall Creek Bridge as one of the fastest Indian boys grabbed the third. Nick handed the reins of one to Jim as he came into view, and the two of them rode back to the starting line.

However, Sir William held up the race and walked directly toward Nick. Nick held his breath as the great man approached him and would have toppled off the horse if Sir William hadn't given him a smile as he quickly said, without giving Nick a chance to reply, "I want a word with you, boy. I could use a smart fellow like you. Come see me next week, and I'll work out a spot for you, and if you're willing to work, someday you'll tower above other men." The wise Sir William was quick to see that Nick was more clever than most.

The race was imminent, giving Nick little chance to consider Sir William's offer, but he was filled with new satisfaction to think that he had been noticed by the greatest man of his time, Sir William Johnson, Baronet of Johnstown. Little did he know, at the time, that the untimely death of Sir William was to dash any chance of his becoming a protegé of the great man.

Nick's friend, Jim, easily won the backward race for, as Nick soon found out, he had given him Sir William's fastest horse. Nick also conceded that Jim's long legs helped him to hold on as they jostled, seated backwards, on the horses.

Sir William declared Nick the winner of the foot races after two hours of competition which left Nick tired and breathless from several close finishes with the best of the Indian runners. His prowess during the day's events had placed him in new stead with his red friends, and he held their respect for many years thereafter.

Nick was in no mood to join the ugliest face contest even though no one enjoyed a good laugh more than he did. His aches and his tiredness slowed him down, and he came to the realization that he was hungry. He stepped into the nearby woods to retrieve his lunch and to enjoy a moment of relaxation away from the crowd. The combination of his mother's good lunch and the solitude of the wooded glen combined to fill Nick's aching body with renewed spirit and he returned to the festivities just in time to listen to the singing contest.

The worst song contest usually closed the sports' day events at Johnson Hall and was immediately followed by the announcing of the grand prize winner and the awarding of prizes.

The Indians sang in their own language and in English and laughed fully and heartily at each, more so at their singing than at the words of the songs. Sir William also indicated his enjoyment of the contest by laughing readily as each contestant sang. Nick joined in with his hearty laugh.

Before Nick knew it, all eyes were upon him, as it apparently became his time to sing. Nick was never at a loss when it came to a good time, and he stood in the center of the group and sang his worst song.

The Indians had sung of famine and disease and of

lack of game, of loss of land and the loss of their elders to the happy hunting grounds. Nick knew that in order to win the contest he would have to use his imagination to think of something greater than any of these. He recalled the old days on the New York docks and the tales the sailors told of the great wars in Europe, and how they said that it was the worst thing that could happen to mankind, and using these he sang his "worst song" —

Oh Baronet, Oh Friend, Use your Great Name
To stop the Bad War that some say will start;
We pray that you will apply your great fame
To end it all before loyalties part.
Father against son — brother to brother
Red men against white men — sad song to sing;
And trouble with the Country called Mother
A war against our Ruler and our King.
Why can't we all think about peace and love?
Let us stay off the battlefield of death.
Can't we tie our strings to the peaceful dove
And continue enjoying freedom's breath
Solve all our differences with common sense
And eliminate war from this day hence?

Little did Nick know that his "worst song" was a prophesy of the great war to come, a war which as the song prophesied would involve all the men in the Stoner family, his close friends, and the Indians. There was no laughter at the end of Nick's song. The thought of war hung in the minds of many, including Sir William Johnson, who hoped that it might all be settled in Boston.

The great man quickly stepped forward and playfully roughing Nick's hair, declared him to be too serious for his age, told him it was too bad he didn't win the horse race, but caught Nick by surprise by wrapping a bearskin around his shoulders and declaring, "Nicholas Stoner, Champion of Johnson Hall."

CHAPTER V

Nick and the Last Council

Little did Nick know, in his youthful ignorance, that the day's festivities were actually one means of keeping the Indians occupied as the wise Superintendent of Indian Affairs delayed their impending council. The pressure of the six hundred tribesmen at Johnson Hall made it difficult, and necessary, to hope that something would happen to ease the situation. Sir William, his former drive failing, hoped for relief from the tense situation.

The violations of the Fort Stanwix treaty, establishing boundaries between the Indian lands and those available to the white man, had increased, and the Indians were beginning to question the great Warraghingagey. Sir William could not justify the killing of such great Indians as Bold Eagle and Silver Heels, who had served faithfully as allies of the King. The Baronet was without prejudice himself and envisioned the day when red and white brothers could live together peacefully and intermarry until they were no longer separate. He knew that the great land of America would one day be shared completely by the two races.

Nick knew that Sir William was not feeling well and wondered why the great man stepped forth to conduct the council meeting himself. Surely there was another who could do as well! But there wasn't. The commanding dignity of Sir William Johnson, the stout, warm heart, the veteran of many fair and firm dealings with the Indians, singled him out as the only man for the hour. And Sir William knew it. His health was bad, and he should be on the Long Island seashore seeking relief from his chronic infirmity, but his capacity for hard work, his unfaltering sense of justice and his strong but never-ceasing sympathy for the Indians caused him to see his duty, as on July 8 he began the council meeting.

Nick's curiosity and interest got the best of him, and he quickly sought permission from his parents to stay in town, spending the nights sleeping under the stars. He listened sadly and intently as the Indian leaders told of the white man's crimes and the loss of their lands. He listened as the Senecas and Cayugas protested against the settlements on the Ohio beyond the treaty lines, as they protested the hostile attitude of the frontiersmen, as they protested against the introduction of rum, as they protested the competition in their trade, and as they protested against the shortage of goods caused by unfair trading practices. This, then, was the task facing the Baronet of Johnstown. Nick watched sympathetically as the ailing Sir William Johnson attended all the sessions and sat around the council fire with his Indian brothers. Nick was more than happy, when on Sunday, the tenth of July, he was allowed to sit with Sir William as he held individual talks with the Indian war chiefs. Nick marked this as the beginning of his knowledge and understanding of the minds of his red friends. And he was thrilled when on the eleventh, a hot breathless summer day, he was present to see the influential Superintendent of Indian Affairs rise once again before the great Sachems to try to justify his white brothers' actions and to ask the great Indian nations for patience and peace.

The councils were always long and tedious with the greatest of the Indian orators making the formal presentations of their complaints or requests and Sir William making lengthy pronouncements and decisions in return. Sir William eloquently told the Indians that the crimes committed against them were the work of individuals who would be punished by the King when they were sought out and caught. He reminded the Senecas that he had given a prisoner over to them; he reminded them, by mentioning The Claim Belt of Alliance and Friendship, that they had been guilty, at one time, of acts against the frontiersmen; he presented them with a new trading policy agreeing to rid them of unwanted traders; and he again asked them to keep peace and to refrain from attacking the settlers until the King could act on his report of the white man's crimes. The Baronet had learned much of the Indian ways, and for two hours he vigorously presented his case, stamping the ground, passing out wampum to emphasize a point, and using all his skill as an orator as he tried to hide the fact that he was not well. Every word was an effort for the great man, and it soon proved to be too much of an effort. As he closed with his summary, "I advise you to put a stop to such evils in time, and you may rest assured that everything in our power will be done to restore peace and afford you satisfaction where you have a claim to it," the lord of Johnson Hall was seized with a severe spasm, always more severe in the heat of summer, and was removed to his bedroom, where within two short hours he uttered, facing responsibilities to the end, "Joseph, control thy people; I am going away."

Nick was saddened by the passing of such a great personage from his world. He spent the next few days dreamingly listening to the chants of the Mohawks for their beloved shepherd, The Great Warraghingagey. All across the Mohawk Valley the high wailing of the great tribes and the cries of the mourning told of the passing of the great Warraghingagey who would no longer enjoy the gliding streams and shadowy forest of his beloved land. Nick went through the motions of the funeral conducted by the Rev. Stewart from Fort Hunter, along with two thousand others, as they marched mournfully to St. John's Church in Johnstown, the bearers in white gloves, white scarves and crapes, and the Sachems of both Mohawk Indian villages wrapped in black shroud blankets, crapes, and wearing black gloves. Nick knew that his world would never be quite the same now that Sir William was gone, and he agreed with Pastor Moseley, who wisely stated in his message to the Rev. Stewart, "Sir William Johnson has given inestimable service to his land and people and the gap left behind by his departing can never be truly filled — the greatest man of our time has resigned his soul to the great and merciful God who made it, and through the merits of our Lord and Savior Jesus Christ, has reached his joyful resurrection to life eternal following his earthly life of sacrifice to the public."

PART III

NICHOLAS STONER
The Patriot

CHAPTER VI

Nick Joins His Country

Nick spent his early teen years listening to the tales of war and the frontiersmen's fear of the Indian scalping knife. His mother had listened quietly to the news of the growing conflict and soon decided that the frontier was too dangerous for her family. She persuaded Henry to make arrangements for the move to Johnstown, and during the summer of 1777, they left the land which Nick considered home.

Nick tried to live in the midst of civilization but each day felt the strong, unexplainable, inner yearning to escape from the pressures of population. He didn't like the lack of privacy in his own back yard; he didn't like the noise and activity of people living side by side; and he didn't like the lack of room to roam.

Henry and Catherine saw the uneasiness in their son. His usual humorous, cheerful, fun-loving self had become quick-tempered and withdrawn. They began to think that the move to the village was a big mistake.

But good fortune came to the Stoners in the guise of the Fisher brothers of the Mohawk Valley. They were in for supplies and looking for a young lad, about Nick's age and with Nick's wilderness experience, to help them with their growing farm chores. Henry talked it over with the anxious men and arranged everything before breaking the news to Nick.

Of course, Nick was delighted to return to the country although he felt somewhat reluctant to leave his family, knowing that he probably could never return to "city" life.

Nick found his new home to be filled with hard work and excitement. The Fisher brothers, John and Harmanus, were staunch patriots and soon filled Nick with the same love and devotion to his country that they held — causing the young Nick to burn with the desire to be of service.

Nick remembered his earlier exposure to the Valley patriots. His father had taken him to Caughnawaga, where three hundred patriots were showing their support of the April 18, 1775, Lexington fighters. It was Nick's first taste of the actual split between friends and neighbors, and he was full of doubts about which group was right. The Patriots had gathered at Caughnawaga to erect a liberty pole. Nick was surprised to note the arrival of Guy and John Johnson, nephew and son of his idol, Sir William, along with Daniel Claus and a troop of armed levies.

Nick also witnessed the first clash in the Mohawk Valley as John Johnson began to harangue the group much as an angry father would scold his sons, telling them to go home and not to fight the crown. His attitude and opinion only served to antagonize the group, especially young Jacob Sammons, who began to yell, "Liar, traitor." It wasn't long before the Johnsons gave the signal, and young Jacob was knocked to the ground by a couple of the roughest levies while the others were held at bay with loaded rifles. It was Nick's first touch with the hatred of men brought on by such a difference of opinion. It was frightening to the young Nick but had planted the seed of his desire to be a part of it.

For the next two years Nick had heard a lot of talk among the valley residents concerning the trouble in Boston and other parts of the country. He had heard arguments between brothers and fathers and sons but he knew that when the time came most would attach themselves to the cause of liberty. Nick had joined his father along with the Fisher brothers at a meeting of the Committee of Safety in Stone Arabia in May of 1775 where, after much discussion, the brave group signed the agreement with the Continental Congress, approved the Boston Tea Party, and sent a document to Albany. Many of the local judges, town officials, and even the Johnson family were opposed to this action and tried to keep these sons of liberty loyal to the crown. Nick, guided more by emotion and imagination than careful thought, admired the bravery of the group in opposing the existing power structure and vowed all the more to watch for his chance to be of service.

Nick also made the journey to Dow Fonda's tavern near Caughnawaga to view some 3,000 militia men assembled to meet Philip Schuyler, who was coming up from Albany with 2,000 men to talk to John Johnson about disarming. General Herkimer also joined the group with 1,000 volunteers. The total force of 6,000 held a grand review on the flats and the frozenMohawk — the largest body of soldiers ever assembled in the valley, certainly an impressive sight for the young Nick!

And it wasn't long before Nick got his chance to serve. He had journeyed to Johnstown, now a military post, to get some news for his friends and to visit his family. The presence of soldiers and horses and army music only heightened the boyish, yet truly patriotic, wish of Nick to serve his country. He noted the recruiting broadside nailed on the jailhouse door calling for the raising of eighty-eight battalions to serve during the war with Great Britain. He also noted with interest that besides the pay and issuance of clothes, a further encouragement of one hundred acres of land would be given at the end of the war. Nick dreamed of having land of his own — having land in the great northern wilderness, up to this point, had been beyond the hopes of the young woodsman.

Nick had a good ear for music, and with a little checking around, he found that Captain Tim Hughes, New York company, needed a fifer. Nick talked it over with his brother John, or better yet, talked John into it, and they both decided to join up. John ended up with Captain Wright as a drummer.

Henry Stoner, with the anxious urging of his worried wife and to end his own concern, decided that he, too, should follow his sons into service. Fortunately, they ended up in the same regiment so that he could keep his eye on the boys and give them fatherly guidance when needed. Besides, Henry, always a man of conviction, would never have forgiven himself if he hadn't joined the cause to throw off oppression.

Nick received an early initiation to war as they journeyed up the Mohawk Valley to Fort Stanwix the very next month. Nick had heard how General Herkimer was ambushed as he marched to lift the British siege of the fort. St. Leger had wisely sent the Johnsons ahead to ambush the untrained group of patriots, who had answered the muster call, in the valley at Oriskany. Herkimer, directing the troops with a shot of lead in his leg, and the eventual withdrawal of the Indians and the British, made Nick think only of the glory of war.

Passing the site of this terrible battle of Oriskany, Nick anxiously went over the small knoll and down to the site of the ambush only to be met with the unbearable stench and horrible sight of his dead heroic countrymen rotting in the sun. As Nick surveyed the swollen bodies and scalped heads, he felt ten years older. He lost his

boyish love of the excitement of being a soldier and re-
solved to take the conflict more seriously and pray for
its early conclusion. Even though young in years, as
with any true lover of peace, Nick was unable in his own
mind to justify war and the loss of a single human life
for any reason. He now was able to understand why the
old sailors dreaded the horrors of war and why, from the
day a war started, men began to search for peace.

CHAPTER VII

Nick Almost Killed

The brave, yet rash, General Arnold had led the body of New York troops directly into the Hessian Camp at Bemis Heights, and Nick knew that if they got out of this alive it would be one of God's miracles. The shot was raining all around them like hail on a hot summer day. Nick and his buddy, Bob Tyrrell, were running shortly behind General Arnold, shooting as they went. Nick having put aside his fife during this engagement, was pausing to reload when the General's horse suddenly bolted upright with his large glassy eyes reflecting the pain he felt. In the same instant he dropped dead to the ground with the General trapped beneath. A wounded Hessian lying nearby raised his rifle and fired point blank at the General, hitting him in the leg. Nick would have killed the Hessian on the spot but the sympathetic General shouted, "He's a fine fellow — don't hurt him!"

The Hessians fought, even though wounded, because their leaders told them that the Americans were without mercy. Upon hearing Nick approach, the wounded Hessian threw down his gun and died at Nick's feet. Nick was about to rush to his General when he heard Tyrrell shout, "Get down, Nick," and a shattering stillness erupted in Nick's head as he fell senseless to the ground, not knowing that a direct hit had shattered the skull of his friend, Tyrrell, close behind him. It was because of this moment in Nick's life, when, as he pondered over the incident later on, he felt that he had been given another chance, and the loss of hearing in his right ear served as a lifetime reminder that he was privileged to have his life. In his heart, Nick knew that the bullet which had shattered his friend Tyrrell's head was meant for him. The knife-like pieces of skull that penetrated his own head and severely injured his right ear could have been fatal. Even his own comrades could have given him up as dead.

However, as is usual in the comradeship of soldiers, Captain Timothy had missed the friendly young fifer and he had sent Sgt. Sweeney to locate him and to bring him back. Sweeney was a brave man, and he liked Nick, but the cannon shot forced his return empty-handed. As he reported to Colonel James Livingston with typical Irish seriousness, "Colonel — a goose just laid an egg there, and you don't catch me to stay there," and he pointed over his shoulder to the general area where Nick still lay unconscious.

Lieutenant Bill Wallace, who counted Nick among his best men, overheard the report and quickly braved the barrage to find Nick, looking mightily close to death, lying on the decapitated body of Tyrrell, covered with bones and blood. Closer examination revealed that Nick still breathed, although the brim of his hat contained a hole a quarter of the size of a nine-pound shot.

Nick rallied enough to recognize his lieutenant and to gain some realization of what had happened. He felt sick all over to think that the life of his companion had been snuffed out so suddenly. It was the first real sadness of his life and he didn't know quite how to handle it. He was helpless.

However, from this point on, Nick vowed to live his own life to the fullest as it suddenly became more precious to him than ever before. Nick carried the burden of Tyrrell's death in his mind throughout his life and was known to console himself by repeating to all who asked what happened, "Bob didn't know what hit him."

Nick was carried, half dazed, along with the wounded Peter Conyne and other injured Americans, to a boat, which immediately departed from Stillwater to Albany on the Hudson. Nick remembers, in between periods of unconsciousness and pain, the fast-moving, tree-covered river banks.

Colonel Frederick Fish waited for Nick in Albany and took him home to Johnstown, where he was cared for by regiment surgeon, Dr. Thomas Reed. The kindly surgeon reluctantly told Nick that he had lost the hearing in one ear, but Nick, still deeply saddened by the death of his buddy, accepted the news without emotion. Nick later noted that a great sadness can overshadow the usual worries of life.

CHAPTER VIII

Nick's Father Is Wounded

Nick recovered quickly, and being anxious to get back with the troops, he was sent to Rhode Island to rejoin his father and brother. He was overjoyed at the chance to be near his family, but as sometimes bad luck follows bad luck, his father was wounded by a musket ball in his head.

The news that his father was wounded filled the young soldier with an insecure feeling of helplessness. As long as he knew his father was engaged in the same skirmishes and action, Nick felt that nothing could happen, that he had someone to turn to, that he felt the security one has when he knows father is there. But now, he knew that he would have to fight the impending tears of helplessness and frustration and become a soldier on his own strength and determination.

Nick reached the medical tent just in time to find his father breathing erratically. The doctor in charge told Nick that his father had a musket ball imbedded in his head and would probably die if the doctors tried to remove it. Nick quickly inquired as to his father's chances if it were not removed immediately and found the answer the same.

But Nick was a stubborn lad and wasn't ready to give up his father so easily. He told the doctor that he had great faith in and admiration for the surgeon's ability and wanted him to take the chance of removing the musket ball. Nick ran quickly with a prayer on his lips to get some silver to fill the hole in Henry's scalp as the doctor skillfully removed the threatening ball.

Nick's fight for his father's life paid off, and it wasn't long before Henry was joyfully showing off the musket ball and telling the story to all who would listen. He always concluded his story with a wink, "I couldn't give up — I had to stay to watch my boys."

CHAPTER IX

Nick the Captive

Up to this time, other than his father's close brush with death, Nick had enjoyed the adventures and exciting parts of war but had often thought about being captured and tortured. The idea made him shudder and feel sick all over. He felt that he could never bear the slow death of torture and often vowed that he would rather die than be captured.

But it happened suddenly! Nick had been involved in two brief skirmishes with the British at the end of the summer and early autumn in Rhode Island and had become more of a rifleman than a fifer. He was the brunt of a little humor from his co-patriots because, as they said, "Nick, that gun is bigger than you are."

It was nearing evening, and the group was resting on an old roadway, protected on both sides by stone walls, laboriously constructed by a hard-working farmer to confine his herd or protect his fields. Halting an approaching group of soldiers, Nick heard, "Don't shoot. We are your own men!" Nick had great faith in mankind and had never been exposed to the treachery often present in men, especially during wartime. Nick dropped his rifle butt to the ground but, almost at the same time, seeing the white belts of the enemy, realized that the approaching group was unfamiliar. There was no time to shoot so with a shout, "Run, the British are upon us!" Nick bolted for the opposite wall, dragging his rifle behind him.

The ancient wall, built of field stone, was composed of as many round stones as flat. As luck would have it, it was upon one of the former that Nick's fleeting foot landed, and it rolled, throwing Nick heavily upon the wall. The British quickly pounced upon him and were ready to shoot when a tall British grenadier raised Nick up exclaiming, "Why, it's only a child, and his rifle is bigger than he is!" Nick didn't mind his buddies making a joke about his size, but he resented being a brunt of the enemies' laughter; whereupon they soon found that it took four of them to subdue the angry fifer.

It wasn't long before most of the others were rounded up by the sneaky British force, and soon Captain Hughes and his men were "out of the war." Nick quickly counted the group and noted that three must have escaped. However, as they huddled together waiting for a boat to pick them up, he overheard his British captor, a John McGaffee, assure the others that one of the Americans has "escaped the troubles of life altogether." Many of the captives counted this man lucky. Most preferred the sudden death on the battlefield to the agony and brutality of prison life. They had heard from other soldiers who had been prisoners that the conditions were indescribable and that many died of starvation and disease. The thought passed through Nick's mind that the British prisoners were luckier than the colonists — the good General Washington had ordered that they be treated with humanity!

Once they were on the boat, Nick settled down to think things over. He continually fought the lump in his throat and was somewhat thankful that the others were captured with him. He hoped that there would be safety in numbers, and maybe they wouldn't be tortured. As Nick thought things over he began to sip from his canteen and unconsciously noted that they had been issued rum before the last skirmish, and he had saved his to pass along to one of the others if they wanted it.

Suddenly, the one called McGaffee grabbed him roughly and yanking the canteen from him guzzled it down. Nick saw no value in protesting further and simply caught the empty canteen as his British counterpart threw it down. Nick unthinkingly tossed it over his shoulder into the water. The loud splash alerted a British officer who nervously threatened to behead Nick with his sword. Nick was saved only by the quick action of the somewhat inebriated McGaffee who stumbled between Nick and the officer.

Nick figured he couldn't come any closer to death and soon stopped worrying about torture. Mumbling a brief prayer for help, he dozed off to a much needed sleep.

Nick jumped quickly, and unfastening his horn from his belt, began to play reveille. However, the sudden noise brought him to his senses, and he soon realized that he was in an island prison camp and that the first of many morning roll calls had begun. Apparently, the small intake of rum had served to give him a good night's sleep, and he had been dragged from the boat to his prison lodgings by his comrades.

Nick soon learned that the prison was located on Conanicut Island, near Rhode Island. The bad reputation of the camp was borne out during the slow-moving, suffering winter months. When summer came again, Nick was ready to break out or be killed. He had found that confinement was unnatural for man, and he vowed that he would never think of war as an adventure again. Nick didn't like what war did to man or what it made them do.

The two men who had escaped at the time of capture had noted where the British had taken their comrades and had been working incessantly for their release. They had decided that the island location made escape impossible and had turned their attention to an exchange plan. It had taken exactly six months and the capture of some important British troops to get the enemy to agree, but the exchange of prisoners was finally arranged, and the great day came. Nick remembered in later years that it was the happiest day of his life, and he was forever grateful for the chance to live out his life without others telling him what to do.

CHAPTER X

Nick the Fifer

Nick's major job in the army was to play the fife, and as the hostilities continued he gained in fame and recognition. Nick enjoyed music, and his own spirit was reflected in the music he played. There were times, however, when Nick's heart wasn't in the job he had to do.

Such was the case in the autumn of 1780. Nick had been on duty in the Hudson Valley and was called upon to serve as a fifer of the guard at Tappan. It was an honor to be chosen, but Nick wasn't sure that he would enjoy the occasion. It was well-known that the noted spy, Major Andre, was to be hanged. Nick thought that it was tragic that two fine men, Andre and Benedict Arnold, should ruin their lives because of this unfortunate war.

Nick arrived early for his unpleasant duty and noted that the gallows were already constructed of white oak crotches and a cross piece with the bark still on. The thought crossed his mind that it was a sad use indeed for such a beautiful tree.

Nick felt a little hungry, and stopping a stranger along the way, he inquired about some food. The stranger introduced himself to the friendly Nick as Elijah Cheedle and directed him to a spot near the gallows where an old woman was selling pies. They both agreed that a homemade pie would taste mighty good and soon offered the huckstress $100 in continental money for apple or pumpkin.

She met their offer with a laugh but finally conceded, "My children, the pie is worth more than the money, but I will take it that I may be able to say, I sold a pie for one hundred dollars."

Nick enjoyed this little respite with Mr. Cheedle, and during the course of the conversation he filled the kindly man full of tales of the beauty and advantages of living in the foothills of the great mountains; so much so, that following the war Mr. Cheedle journeyed to Johnstown and settled at Kingsborough himself. Nick knew that he could live in no other spot in the world and had a knack of conveying this feeling and his own enthusiasm to others. He told his new-found friend about the woodland trails. He described the early morning, mist-filled, forest glades and the moonlight over a mountain lake. He talked of the Sacondaga and the Mohawk. He mentioned the tasty trout and venison stew. And he tried to explain the renewal of a man's spirit after a jaunt into the mountain wilderness. Nick just knew that it was the best place in the world to live.

Nick was called, and the guard assembled at the prison to escort the doomed spy to the gallows. Nick marched smartly and played his best with the soldiers of the guard, but he could never admit to anyone that it was a spectacle worth repeating. He watched the brave Major Andre march to his death with high courage and unshakable nerve. He wondered, for the moment, if he felt worse about the whole incident than the prisoner. Nick could only question in his mind, as men went about the affairs of war, who are we to snuff out a life and silently say to himself, "Judge not that ye be not judged."

Nick remained in the middle of the action throughout the war. His duty at Yorktown enabled him to witness the siege and the surrender of General O'Hare. He served as a fifer under General Lafayette. His regiment under Colonel Cortland took five hundred prisoners for some distance on their return march.

The war never changed Nick's honest approach to

life. He was always trying to do good and sometimes became the brunt of jealousies and displeasures of the other men. Nick often found that old-fashioned goodness made others uneasy.

Just such an occurrence took place on the ferry crossing at York. Nick saw a French officer drop his purse, and although advised by his cronies to pocket the money and say nothing, Nick, unable to follow any but the right course, searched out the officer and returned the purse to him.

The expressive Frenchman was overwhelmed with joy at the return of his money and exclaiming, "You pe a grand poy! You pe bon honest American," he presented Nick with a half doubloon ($8) for a reward. Nick received a lot of pleasure from being honest yet knew that he could be no other way. He realized that if he kept the money he would feel like a thief and experience many sleepless nights. Anyway, he shared his reward with his buddies and they "forgave" him for being so honest.

CHAPTER XI

Nick Stationed at Home

Nick couldn't have been happier. Winter was coming on, and the camp rumor indicated that the troops were being reduced and combined, and his outfit was being assigned to Captain Samuel T. Pell. Everyone knew, unofficially of course, that Captain Pell was to march to Schenectady and to winter quarter at the frontier station in Johnstown. That meant home for Nick, a chance to see his family and friends. He surely missed his mother, although, as a false sign of manhood, he tried not to admit it even to himself. In fact, Nick thought he might even get a chance to get into his beloved wilderness to hunt and fish.

And hunt and fish he did! The official word came in due time, and by late fall the troops were busily engaged at Johnstown trying to keep the frontier inhabitants safe from the raiding parties of the enemy. And Nick was busily engaged in supplying the troops with forest game.

Nick found that the officers would pay well for the products of the wilderness. Along with a few friends, he was able to keep busy hunting and fishing. Nick felt fortunate, indeed, to earn money doing what he liked best.

The work wasn't without danger, however, as Nick soon found out. Nick, along with three friends, Charles Worth, Charles Darby, and John Foliard, were busily fishing the Cayadutta (Muddy Creek) near Johnson Hall. Suddenly, to the surprise of the group, Darby took off in the direction of the Hall as though he had seen a ghost. Looking around, the boys spied a party of In-

dians emerge from a patch of hemp near the hall barn.
The Indians began firing at the boys, who quickly made
their escape through the woods. Years of learning how to
move in the wilderness again saved the life of young Nick
along with those of his friends who followed his example.

Returning to the barracks, the boys soon learned that
they had been attacked by a group of Tory spies in dis-
guise who needed a prisoner to prove that they had
been in Johnstown. Nick later discovered that Thomas
Hunter, a seventy-year-old resident of Scotch Bush, was
taken to Canada by the enemy. Nick counted his blessings that he himself wasn't captured again, but was also
relieved when the old man was later returned unharmed
to his home.

Nick's Aunt Barbary lived near the fort with her husband, Conrad Reed, who baked for the garrison. The
boys liked to visit their aunt and uncle even though their
father had disapproved because of the leaning of his
brother-in-law towards the royalty. Nick himself recalled one night during a visit a rap on the window; his
uncle disappeared through a trap door to the cellar, and
his aunt left the house. She returned shortly with several
gaudy handkerchiefs for the Tory ladies whose husbands
or lovers were in Canada.

Telling his story at the garrison one winter evening,
Nick received a good explanation. One of the men had
learned, while visiting at Fon Clair's or Jim Burke's
Tavern, that Joe Howell, a loyalist living between Johnstown and Sacondaga, had missed the chance to capture
Nick. He, along with a small party of the enemy, had
visited the settlement as spies and had seen Nick through
his aunt's window. They had a pre-arranged signal and
had called her out to discuss Nick's capture. Barbary,
showing her love for her likeable nephew, had convinced

the group that Nick's capture would ruin their family, and her husband would lose his baker's job and be unable to spy on the soldiers. Howell would have liked to have held Nick as proof of his accomplished mission and would have kept him in a Canadian prison. Again Nick was thankful that he had avoided capture. He also decided to be more cautious and try to be less trusting of his fellowman in the future — a difficult task for the friendly Nick.

CHAPTER XII

Nick's "Pigeon" Hunting

Nick's reputation as a hunter was widespread. However, when Nick was not hunting, he was a sociable boy and counted as many women friends among his acquaintances as he did men friends. He enjoyed the company of women if for no other reason than he liked to joke and talk, and he could always count on his women friends to be a good audience.

Nick was often seen by his friends in the company of womenfolk, especially the two Brouse girls who lived some distance from the fort on the main highway. Knowing this, Jim Dunn had told Captain Pell, as something of a joke on his friend Nick, that Nick hunted two kinds of "pigeons." Whereupon, Captain Pell persuaded Nick to take him "hunting."

Nick obliged, reluctantly, because this would cause him to pass, during the evening courting hours, the home of the Jeremiah Masons, who had a dark-eyed daughter, Anna. And Nick was quite partial to Anna. In fact, she had warned him, when pigeon hunting, to stay away from that Tory house, the Brouse's!

But Nick, not being entirely against the idea, came up with a plan that would meet the challenge. He obtained an old white horse. Leaving their shooting irons behind, he trotted off with Captain Pell behind him on the horse. About a mile from the fort, he took a detour off the main highway so as not to pass Anna's house; whereupon the old horse stumbled, threw the two "hunters" into the brush; and trotted riderless toward Anna's home. The two then proceeded quickly on foot to see the girls.

They joined the Brouse girls in separate rooms by some prearranged tactics of the girls. Nick heard the Mason's dog barking furiously, but he felt secure in the thought that it must be barking at the old white horse, and he assumed that he had gone by unnoticed. He did, however, feel a slight tinge of guilt for being a party to such a sly undertaking.

Nick quickly put the thought aside and turned his attention to the routine chatter of his hostess for the night. Polly was busily engaged in telling him how long it had been since he had "come a calling," how nice it was of him to bring the handsome Captain Pell to see her sister, and how she had heard so much about his escape from the Tories behind Johnson Hall. This kind of talk began to make the somewhat self-centered Nick feel a little more relaxed and kindly toward the girl.

The sudden thought crossed Nick's mind that he was alone with Polly; for some reason, unknown to him, it was a frightening moment. Nothing in his past had prepared him for this moment — a moment when he was in a woman's presence not knowing what his intentions might be or what he would do during the coming hours.

Nick allowed his gaze quickly to engulf Polly in her entirety in a feeble attempt to scrutinize her thoughts. He gained nothing by this except to notice the fullness of her womanly figure as she bent slightly to remove her shoes.

Nick, trying to pull his gaze away, nervously placed one hand in his pocket fingering a York shilling he had earned that afternoon by proving his marksmanship. He impulsively pulled it out and asked, in a feeble attempt to show he was a man of the world — "Do men ever pay you for your favors?" Polly stiffened, and Nick knew at once that he had asked the wrong question. In an attempt to right himself, he broke into his usual wide grin and playfully dropped the York shilling into the opening at the top of her dress. "Why, Nicholas Stoner," she exclaimed with shock and amazement but also with a slight trace of amusement in her voice.

Nick relaxed a bit and deemed it a good joke until Polly turned the tables on him and announced — "Now it's up to you to get it out."

She stood directly in front of him with her hands on her hips and her bare feet slightly spread apart, and Nick knew that he had met his match. Her quick comeback and that gnawing attraction he felt continued to make him uneasy. But Nick was a good sport and accepted each challenge as it came. He quickly turned her around, put his arms around her middle, grabbed a handful of her garments and quickly shook it until the clank of the shilling was heard on the floor. Polly let out a small scream which made Nick jump but resulted in both bursting into a laughing spell until they dropped, exhausted, onto the bed.

The sudden quietness and the closeness of the two again caused Nick to feel ill at ease, but as he looked deeply yet timidly at Polly's beautiful eyes, she wrapped her small white arms gently around his neck and kissed him long and full and lovingly on the lips — and Nick's heart and mind rested — and he knew that he could no longer think of his womenfolk as simply an audience for his levity and entertainment.

Nick was ready to call it a night before he became more involved, but knowing Captain Pell, it was evident that it would be useless to try to initiate the homeward journey. He also knew that before the night was over he would probably disappoint Polly. A long time ago, with his father's guidance, he had promised himself that he would not become intimately involved with any woman unless she was his wife. He resigned himself to accepting the attention of the affectionate girl throughout the night and had to admit he enjoyed holding her close and to his surprise, he also enjoyed kissing her. This bothered him a little because he knew full well he wasn't her first boy friend. Nick was also surprised to find that Polly seemed to relax in his company and actually seemed relieved that he didn't force his attentions on her. He found that this was true, and one of his friends told him, "Polly says that you're the only gentleman that ever called on her!"

Nick was able to break away even though Polly objected, because he again heard the barking of Mason's dog. The thought crossed his mind that some enemy spies were in the area and that he and his Captain would bring scandal and dishonor to his country to be killed or captured in such a situation. In fact, they were completely defenseless, having left their arms at the garrison. Nick alerted Captain Pell and conveyed some urgency in his voice to stir the captain to action so he quickly joined Nick for an observation trip.

The dawn was just lighting the horizon as Nick and Captain Pell began the long walk home. The captain was showing all signs of being a happy man and couldn't say enough about the lovely Julie Brouse and about how soon he would return. Nick just couldn't share his joy, especially while nursing the thought that he had to pass Anna's house to get home.

Another side trip through the underbrush to avoid the Mason house satisfied Nick that he had not been seen by Anna, and he vowed to himself that this was the end of his "pigeon hunting."

CHAPTER XIII

Nick Loses His Girl

Nick felt sick all over. The news had reached him in the strange and mysterious way that bad news has of traveling—the news kept running continuously through his mind. Anna, whom Nick had always considered his own, had married William Scarborough; apparently, Nick felt, she had not expected him to return from the war. All the food that Nick had tried to swallow since he had heard the news was still in his throat. Nick knew that life would no longer be the same for him. How could he go on? Which way could he turn? He was seized by a complete state of helplessness; a sense of inadequacy filled him, a sense he had never before encountered, building up in his throat and stomach until he thought he would burst. He had taken Anna for granted, hardly stopping to realize that he loved her, and now he had lost her.

With clenched teeth, throbbing head, and a strange shortness of breath, Nick wondered why he was so trapped — so filled with the desire for her that he simply couldn't forget this part of his life and retain the ever-present independence of a man of the woods.

But, by his own admission to himself, Nick had to take some action to see her, to talk with her, to convince her to his thinking. However, his mind wasn't as clear as usual, and he was at a loss for the first time in his life.

Nick could see no way to turn except to pray as he did when he was troubled, however, knowing that prayer isn't a magic device that produces immediate results. As he prayed, Nick found his thinking began to clear.

He knew that it was wrong to go to Anna and ask her to leave her new husband. He knew that it was wrong to leave the front and to endanger himself and the others. He knew that he had nothing to offer Anna but the chance that he might get through the war alive or he might not; therefore, Nick prayed for strength—strength to do that which was right, and for peace—peace of mind to forget, assisted by time and faith, that he would again know the happiness found by loving and being loved.

But yet Nick knew that someday Anna would be his —no one could be so desired and so wanted by a man like Nick, who held the firm belief that the good things in life came to those who always tried to do those unselfish and necessary tasks for his fellowman. Nick felt that up to this point in his life he had shared many of the good things, and his discourageless heart gave him the hope to go on. Yes, he knew that Anna would be his, and he vowed to wait patiently for the day when life's events were such that he could hold her close and call her his own.

CHAPTER XIV

Nick Loses His Father

It was the first hoeing of the season. Henry was happy once again to be able to walk between the rows of corn and see the little green stalks poking their way skyward. The early morning sun lengthened their shadows and seemed to be calling them to awake. He judged it a miracle of God that such a tiny seed could, in one season, produce such a large stalk and so many large ears of corn. Henry gained a lot of satisfaction in being a part of such an undertaking. He carefully walked to the far end of the field gazing fondly at the surrounding woods, up at the sunny blue sky with its puffs of pure white clouds, and down at the bright green shoots poking up through the rich brown earth. Little did Henry, a survivor of so many wartime skirmishes, think that tragedy could come to him in such a peaceful setting.

Henry had served his three years in the American Army and, in addition, had taken another man's place for three months. And now he was happy to be home again with his lonely wife. He also was thankful to be discharged in time to get the crops in. He had moved to a farm in the town of Amsterdam, hoping to avoid having to clear ground for crops and thereby losing part of the growing season. He knew what a job it was to clear the wilderness for crops and didn't want to waste part of the growing season in doing so. The season was short enough already with frost in May and September. Henry had lost many a crop to an early frost.

At the same time the elder Mr. Stoner was counting his blessings and chopping up the dirt and weeds around his corn, a party of seven Indians from Canada was traveling through the Mohawk Valley trying to capture a noted judge, William Harper, or John Littel, who later became sheriff. They had failed in their mission and were overjoyed to learn from the Tory, Andrew Bowman, that a Whig, Henry Stoner, lived nearby and that he had two sons still in the army. Such a capture or killing would more than fulfill the mission of this unworthy group.

Mr. Stoner's nephew, Michael Reed, joined him in the garden just as Mrs. Stoner blew the horn for breakfast. Looking up, young Reed was the first to see two of the redskins charging out of the woods. His yell sent the elder Stoner loping for the house to grab his loaded rifle.

The nimble Indians skirted the flax field and cut Nick's aging father off before he reached the house. Henry decided to surrender in order to protect the boy and his wife. Raising his hands he offered himself to the savages. Basically, Henry was a peace-loving man and sought to avoid trouble whenever possible. He knew that any act of retaliation against the savage group would stir them to anger; therefore, he believed that his peaceful stance would calm them down. But the savage group, disappointed in the original mission and filled with the hatred brought on by war, had other ideas. They didn't want a peaceful old man to take back to Canada.

The scalpers knew no mercy. Planting a tomahawk in the scalp of the defenseless man, they grappled for the evidence of the poor man's death which would bring a lot of British gold. It was noted later that the greedy Indians had also taken the piece of silver that covered Henry's old scalp wound. Little wonder that the peaceable Nick was unable to refrain from vowing to avenge his father's tragic death.

The other Indians ran to the Stoner dwelling, looted it, and set it on fire. Mrs. Stoner was unharmed and was able to escape the burning home with one dress she wisely threw out the back window as the savages approached. She ran to a neighbor's house supposing her husband and nephew to be prisoners.

The traitorous Bowman helped the savages carry the plunder to a hiding place near the Sacondaga along with a prisoner named Palmatier, captured along the way, and the young nephew of Stoner's. During the night, Palmatier was able to escape. Bowman, pretending to be a prisoner, also returned to his home the next night. Young Reed was taken to Canada and forced to serve as a drummer in Butler's Rangers until the end of the war.

Henry's neighbors had immediately gathered together to rescue the old patriot from danger. They journeyed to the Stoner farm only to find the old soldier half dead near the road. The little assistance they could render proved to no avail, and Henry Stoner breathed his last. They buried him beneath a nearby hemlock tree, knowing that it was a suitable location for such a man as Henry, who had loved the woods and gardens in the great outdoors.

The angry group, hearing from Palmatier that Bowman had aided the Indians, went in search of the fiend. Upon his return home they took him to the fortified Johnstown jail. When he wouldn't confess his crimes, they pretended to hang him, even to the point of kicking the barrel out from under him but were unable to get a confession. He was given a stern warning about his future conduct and allowed to go free. Later Nick sent word, on hearing a résumé of his friends' efforts, that Bowman was only living today because the son of Henry Stoner was on duty at Kings Ferry and couldn't get home.

CHAPTER XV

Nick's Joke

Shortly after the war had ended in the spring of 1783, Nicholas Stoner was encamped with the troops near Newburgh. Things were slow around the camp, and the hot, sticky weather settled like a pall on the tired, homesick men. An occasional temper exploded as it reached the breaking point. An air of restlessness surrounded the camp like a fog; a restlessness born of homesickness and desire for families. Camp conditions and the terrible times of the war cause men to feel the inner torment of trouble. As in any group of comparable size and condition, one man is compelled to keep up the spirits, to make an attempt at humor, no matter how futile. The man in this instance was Nick Stoner. Nick wanted others to be happy, and he always enjoyed a good prank.

Nick had just finished playing a tune on his fife and was seated with the others on a circle of fallen logs and large glacier-left rocks, exchanging stories. The group was a mixture of those who came through the war unscathed and those who showed signs of battle. It was obvious to all that "General George," one of the Negro slaves who had joined the Army of the North, was cursed for life by the previous cold winter. His toes had been frozen off while in prison with Nick and the others on Conanicut Island. Also, while there he had gained the name of "General George." He had claimed to be nameless, simply answering to "Hey, you!" up to that time. The men, feeling that he should have a name, had good-naturedly called him "General George" while in prison and had told him that the enemy would think he was their commander and that, if anyone was tortured, he would be the one. The poor fellow didn't appreciate the joke.

It happened, as it sometimes does, that "General George" walked, or rather waddled, by this group during a lull in the conversation, whereupon, without thinking, the witty Nick called out, "Look, here comes a stool pigeon!"

George, burning with rage, grabbed a bayonet and proceeded to charge Nick, who fled for dear life to the nearest building, a hut occupied by Lieutenant Colonel Cochrane, hero of many sudden skirmishes, and his friends.

Nick's lightning-like entrance caused the war-wearied officers to spring to action as if invaded by the enemy army. Drawing their swords they stood ready for the approaching enemy. The immediate entrance of George, waving the bayonet and yelling "tool pigeon" and "deblish musiker" amused the officers who immediately were bent upon suppressing their mirth.

The toeless soldier managed to calm himself enough to blurt out his brief tale of woe.

"That deblish musiker, that deblish musiker — he call me tool pigeon—my po'toes frozed off—I git 'im, I git 'im!"

Lieutenant Colonel Cochrane quickly promised the limping soldier that he would punish Nick, who was prepared to jump out the nearest window if the race continued.

Upon George's departure the entire group burst out laughing, including Colonel Cochrane, who was unable to remain serious any longer. The sudden breaking of the tension, after months of serious wartime decisions, served to send the officers into uncontrolled laughter.

The sensitive Nick, seeing their intense mirth, felt a pang of sympathy for George and repented for his impulsive deed, knowing that he deserved any punishment that Colonel Cochrane would give him. He was released with a short lecture and the threat of a rawhide whipping if he caused any more trouble with his companion. Nick vowed to himself that from that day forth he would think before speaking and do his best to show his friendship for "General George."

CHAPTER XVI

Nick and the Last Battle

The snow began to fall and created a certain excitement among the men, a sort of mixture of happiness and disgust that comes with the first October snowfall of a new winter season. But their arrival at Johnstown quickly ended their attention to the weather. General Cornwallis and the British had surrendered earlier at Yorktown, but Nick knew that Colonel Willert had forced the three-day march from Fort Rensselaer for something more than a practice celebration. The 416 men that he had collected had spent one whole day crossing the Mohawk on hand-made floats, and Colonel Willert's shouting and coaxing for speed indicated that something important was up. The men, tired of war and thinking it was over, were sick of the business of soldiering and were anxious to get home. Nick had heard that Washington believed that to make a good peace, you ought to be well prepared to carry on the war, and, apparently, to carry on the war was to be their job.

Of course, Nick knew and the men knew what was up, as is so often true of wartime secrets. Anna's husband, William Scarborough, had joined the group with the scouts from Johnstown, and he had informed Nick that they had spotted Major Ross along with four companies of the 2nd Battalion of Sir Johnson's regiment of Royal Greens, Major Butler with his Rangers, and enough Indians to make a fighting force of 1,000 men about five miles east of Johnstown, as they came from below Amsterdam. Nick figured that Colonel Willert, instead of waiting at Fort Hunter, was timing his march to come in behind them on the afternoon of October 25, 1781, at Johnstown. This was the country that Nick knew best.

When they arrived, Colonel Willert quickly dispatched Major Rowley and the Tryon County Militia to attack the rear of the enemy forces. He also sent along sixty levies to provide reinforcement if needed. The militia men welcomed the 2-1 odds as being fair to them. They were proud of their powers with the rifle. They set 2 o'clock as the attack time, and it was exactly at 2 o'clock that Nick sounded the bugle charge.

Colonel Willert attacked the surprised 1,000-man force unexpectedly and head-on. His surprise caused Ross to retreat into the woods to the north of Johnson Hall. Pressing his advantage, and with the advice of Nick, who knew well this familiar home territory, Willert rallied his forces together and closed in from all sides. The fresh snow on the ground made it easy to determine the enemy's position. The battle was quick and violent, with the American marksmen scoring with each shot.

The British fled, and the three-hour battle ended as quickly as it started. It was nearing 5 o'clock and with the early twilight hours, Colonel Willert ordered an encampment for the night, rather than a head-long chase into a possible ambush. The men wanted to finish the fight and get some time off to go into Johnstown to celebrate the end of the war, but Colonel Willert quickly squelched their grumbling by organizing a burial party. Thoughts of their dead comrades ended any desire for celebration.

Nick agreed to go along to assist with the burial and to add a little music to the grave-side funeral service. Nearing the hillside bordering on Johnson Avenue, Nick spied a body of one of the scouts laying face-down in the ditch. He quickly rolled him over, to discover that it was William, Anna's husband of only three months. Nick should have been happy because now he might have a chance for his beloved Anna, but as he blinked back the tears, he knew that Bill's tragic death would be a great loss. His brief marriage and, as Nick had heard from Bill the day before, his expected baby now without a father, would be an added sadness for Anna. Nick only hoped that he could be of some help to her during this time of loss and possibly someday a father for her child. He put in a request to go to Johnstown when the battle was over, so that he might tell Anna how her husband had died. In his own mind he could only question why — why was he able to get through the entire war alive while Bill's short effort was only met by death?

The Americans were up at dawn and quickly overtook the retreating enemy at Jerseyfield on the north side of Canada Creek. The death of Walter Butler as he arrogantly taunted the approaching Americans, and the severe losses caused the enemy troop to disperse and dispel as the last battle of the American Revolution came to a happy ending for those in the Mohawk Valley.

PART IV

NICHOLAS STONER
The Man

CHAPTER XVII

Nick Takes a Wife

The torment in Nick's beloved country had ended, and now the torment in Nick's mind began in earnest. The recently widowed Anna was as charming to the discharged Nick as ever, and a day rarely went by when Nick didn't find some excuse to pass by her house or go to see her. And he knew that she still felt an attraction to him that was unchanged by the war and her marriage. He was proud of the Badge of Merit that he had earned for six years of faithful service, and he used it to impress his former sweetheart.

Nick had grown up during his years in service. His six years of tough army life with his older war-time companions had turned the slight, lanky, idealistic boy who joined his country's cause into a man of stature with a new and greater appreciation of life. The Nick who returned from war had reached his full growth of just under six feet. Nick remained slender throughout his life despite his love of eating. His light brown hair was set off by the gold ring still in his ear and the homemade fur cap he usually wore on the top of his head. Nick also retained his forest walk, slightly bent, moving like the inhabitants of the wilderness.

But Nick, although now grown to manhood, still had some boyish notions in his mind. Was he ready to stop keeping company with his other lady friends? Was he ready to settle down for life with one woman, and, more precisely, was Anna the girl for him? When Nick was in Anna's company there was no doubt in his mind that he wanted to share his life with her; yet when he was enjoying the freedom and independence that he found in the woods, uncertainties filled his mind. However, Nick knew that he was a family man. He knew that his own family had instilled in him the kind of life, and love, and security that a good family brings to a man. No, Nick couldn't picture himself going through life without a family around him bringing him joy, giving him attention, and making him feel needed and wanted in the world. Yet, he knew that he had this streak of independence in him that his family would simply have to accept in order to live with him.

The day finally came. Nick and Anna had packed a picnic lunch and spent the morning following the Hall Creek behind Johnson Hall and out toward Scotch Bush. The green, wooded glens, the bright sunshine, and the happy sounds of the birds combined to make Nick feel good all over. He loved the woods; he loved Anna, and to have the two together on such a perfect day was almost too much for a romantic young outdoorsman.

It wasn't long before the two, under the influence of Nick's enthusiasm for the woodlands, were busily engaged in selecting a site for a house and talking about the number of children a family should have and reminiscing about their earlier days together. Nick suddenly made up his mind that Anna was what he wanted — woman was made for man — and he knew that she was for him. Nick always got what he wanted, and it didn't take him long to convince Anna (or had she convinced him), and to make arrangements for her hand in marriage.

It was a good marriage. Nick enjoyed his home, his wife, his four sons, and two daughters. Nick proved to be a good provider and a good helpmeet for Anna around the house.

He took a great deal of pride in being able to keep the house running smoothly even when Anna was sick or away, and he enjoyed teaching his children everything that he could about God's wonderful world.

And Anna proved to be the right companion for the ambitious Nick — ambitious in work, ambitious in love, and ambitious in life. Anna, herself, was most ambitious as a housewife and continued to make Nick proud of her beauty as well as of her cooking and of her house cleaning. Nick would often ask his lovely wife why she put up with such a character as himself and why she didn't marry someone who could give her a better and easier life. But Anna was happy with the one she loved, and Nick knew it, as she gave in to his every whim and desire and made him feel his manhood both in the privacy of his home and in the world about him.

Nick spent forty years living with and loving the beautiful and faithful Anna before she died, and even though he later found another, he retained many happy memories of his life with one so fine.

Chapter XVIII

Nick and the
Tryon County Court House

The triangular iron bell in the copper covered tower of Johnstown's Tryon County Court House could tell many tales of trials and tribulations of the Mohawk Valley and rural mountain folks. Her ancient thick Holland-brick walls, as substantial today as they were in 1772, have heard the famous voices of Alexander Hamilton, Aaron Burr, and Judge Cady, and have held many dramatic and historical moments within her dignified and paneled interior. However, none can match the year 1783 — the year of inspection by General George Washington and the year of her first murder trial. Now deputy sheriff, Nicholas Stoner's life was both involved and affected by these memorable events.

Nick first heard about General Washington's impending visit during his first month on the job. His discharge issued June 8, 1783, was still temporary, reading "The within certificate shall not avail the Bearer as a Discharge until the Ratification of the definitive Treaty of peace; previous to which Time, and until Proclamation thereof shall be made. He is to be considered as being on Furlough. George Washington." The announcement arrived by dispatch from Assistant Quartermaster Dimler. Sheriff Littel showed it to Nick who was filled with excitement. His six years of service brought him to maturity but left him with awe and admiration for his commander-in-chief.

General Washington's journey had taken him from

Newburgh to Albany on July 19 by boat and then by horseback along the Mohawk Valley as far west as Oneida Lake and back along the north shore to Fort Plain, Stone Arabia, and to Johnstown by August 1, 1783. Everywhere the famous General went he was welcomed by flocks of people, the valley soldiers and school children included. He made many speeches thanking and praising them for withstanding the struggle with the British and the Indians and emphasized, time and again, that the course of history was determined by the action in the Mohawk Valley. He stayed in many meager dwellings because of the need for rebuilding following the destruction by the Indians of the valley homes, and he met many who had been prisoners of the formidable foe. The good General expressed nothing but sympathy and admiration for the valley folks who had borne the brunt of the hostilities.

Washington met Nick and the sheriff at the door of the court house and despite the crowd and the urging of the two men, Washington announced his desire to spend the night in Schenectady. He asked Nick, whom he knew to be a veteran, to accompany him on his tour of the court house and to tell him about Johnstown. Nick, always glad to talk about his beloved country, expounded on the advantages of living adjacent to the great wilderness, near the great waterway afforded the Mohawk to the west as well as east, and the fact that some land was still available for purchase. He so impressed the great General, who already had seen the great possibilities for the development of the region, that Washington purchased some land in the mountains which he still held at the time of his death.

The short time in the shadow of the great American hero gained Nick the esteem of his friends and neighbors. He considered the visit of Washington as a high-light of his life and could be counted upon to relate what he "said" and what the General "said" for many years thereafter.

Shortly after Washington's departure, when the legislature began to discuss the renaming of Tryon County in honor of General Richard Montgomery, Nick was preoccupied with an arrest he had made as an obligation to duty and for no other reason. His mind and heart told him that it was wrong, and he determined to do everything that he could do to obtain justice, and justice, in this case, could mean acquitting a murderer.

John Adam Hartmann, a Revolutionary War hero, was charged with killing an Indian. It was said that the Indian was carrying a tobacco pouch made of the skin of the arm and hand of a white child. Feelings ran high among the populous, and Nick knew that he agreed with the majority: the killing was justified, and John Hartmann should be freed. In arresting Hartmann, Nick had to do that which was right, even though the whole town was against him. The rumors, wild and vicious, called Nick everything from an "Indian lover" to a "child hater" — and nothing could be further from the truth. But Nick always did his job.

Nick knew the story well, even before the case opened in court. He thought that there was a lack of evidence, but it had become his duty to make the arrest. John had met the Indian in a tavern on the Fort Stanwix Road. The Indian had been bragging about the scalps he had taken and the women and children he had killed during the war. This kind of talk, true or untrue, was difficult for a Revolutionary War veteran to swallow, and when the Indian produced the pouch made of a child's hand, John could no longer listen to the braggart. Nick knew just how John felt, experiencing the same uncontrollable anger when he thought about the Indian who killed his father.

John, holding his building anger under control, left the tavern only to be joined by the Indian for the journey through the woods to Johnstown. The two entered the woods; only one came out. The Indian was never seen again. It wasn't long before the story circulated, as news did in those days, that John Adam Hartmann had done away with his former foe. However, Nick noted in his report that no body was found and none of the Indian's belongings turned up.

Public opinion swayed back and forth as rumor flourished and testimony became known. At first, John was the villain, having done in a red brother of the forest. Then he was a hero for killing one who would scalp a child. Some reported seeing the Indian after the supposed murder. Some turned in pieces of the Indian's belongings supposedly found in the forest. Arguments were commonplace in local stores and taverns. There were those who said John should be hanged, that no one should get away with murder. Others argued that man should not take another's life, and John should be jailed or set free. Still others claimed that he was innocent.

Nick soon began to note the public opinion was for acquittal. His friends and neighbors felt that the Indian deserved what he got and, anyway, there was no body to prove his death. John himself wisely said nothing. He quietly hung his head and answered only with a nod or a shake or a shrug when questioned. He seemed to be a man without hope, yet at peace with the world. Nick knew John as a good man. Even if he had killed the Indian in a moment of anger, Nick knew that John would feel sorry that it happened. It just wasn't John's nature to do such a thing and forget it.

Judge Cady conducted a serious and strict trial. When onlookers interfered, he cleared the courtroom Where hearsay evidence was introduced, he struck it out. He instructed the jury to disregard the feelings of the public and to weigh the evidence fairly and honestly. He asked them to forget any prejudice they held against the red man and to consider their verdict like any other.

The testimony was short and consisted mainly of establishing the fact of the two men's presence in the tavern, their leaving together, and the disappearance of the Indian. The deliberations were short, and John Adam Hartmann was acquitted and freed for lack of evidence. The body and belongings of the Indian were found in the woods a year later. Nick often questioned himself, "What was justice in this case? Could he walk an inch taller for his part in directly influencing another's life?" It was strange, but he felt that a chip had been taken from his heart for doing a necessary job and thereby losing the friendship of John and his family.

Chapter XIX

Nick's Darkest Hour

When we look upon Nicholas Stoner and his life, we see a man who was a little more intelligent, a little more active, and a little more adventurous than most men of his time. We see one who was as much at ease in the midst of society as he was in the woods. And many said that he knew no fear. It was these characteristics that sometimes led Nick to do, aggressively, that which he thought was right whether others agreed or not. It was impossible for him when he could do the "right" thing to go along with the crowd, even to the point of jeopardizing his own life.

Such was the case on that hot afternoon during the summer of 1785. Nick was serious about his job as deputy sheriff and went out of his way to see that law and order prevailed. There were many occasions when he could have closed his eyes and avoided trouble, but as long as he was on the job he felt that inner fire of righteousness causing him to serve so well that it could never be said of him, "He didn't do his job."

Nick had been busy all day and shortly after the lunch hour was making a routine visit to De Fonclair's tavern, which later became Union Hall, to see a constable who was in the kitchen. Nick had missed lunch so he was in a hurry to get the business done. He had some necessary paper work that went along with the job even though he objected on many occasions. "Paper work interferes with the job," he maintained, and rightly so.

Seven Canadian Indians, apparently hunters, were

engaged in some exuberant drinking at the tavern but were quieted by Nick's entrance and official glance. As a precaution Nick always made it a point to know who was in town. Slapping a York shilling on the table, he joined the group for a drink as was the custom of the day. Nick often wondered why he consumed the terrible beverage — so contrary to his nature. It seemed the thing to do when he wanted to relax and socialize with his cronies or to gain the confidence of strangers. Yet, Nick didn't like the sensation he experienced when he no longer had control over his own emotions and feelings. Years of coping with the wildness of the woods had taught him the value of control over his own mind and actions. He never knew when the loss-of-control feeling would strike — sometimes after two drinks — sometimes it took four and sometimes he wasn't sure how many — but never consistent enough that he could learn his final lesson — for as soon as time and circumstances occurred at the opportune moment Nick was the first to join the fun and to encourage a drink of rum or kill devil or flip — and the first to be sorry later!

(Little did Nick know that today he would be sorry indeed.) He began his questioning in an off-handed fashion. He nonchalantly turned to the lightest-skinned of the group, figuring he would speak English, and asked, "Where you from?"

Immediately, the largest member of the group stepped in and in a threatening manner demanded of Nick, "What business is it of yours?"

It may have been the heat of the day; it may have been the fact that Nick had missed lunch; it may have been the rum, but Nick, cracking the bones in his right hand, exploded with "Out, out, I say!"

Nick knew from his mother's early Bible teaching, a

harsh word stirs up anger, but it was too late. The enraged Indian came at him full force, whereupon Nick dodged, throwing him full length onto the table, breaking and scattering the flasks and bottles. The Indian was a fighter, and the hard fall he took only served to heighten his anger. He again tried to jump the nimble Nick who, this time, remembering his early Indian fights at Johnson Manor, grabbed an intended kick to the hip and attempted to throw the Indian into the fire. He partially succeeded because his opponent landed sitting upright in a large kettle of gravy, severely burning himself and losing all his desire for furthering his fight with Nick.

Nick had a good laugh over it later when he found out that during this foray the tavern owner had gone to Lawyer Annbial Rust, one of Nick's close friends. Lawyer Rust, as a private joke on Nick, had told the owner that the moon affected Nick, and he was certain that the disarranged deputy would pay for the damages later.

The frustrations of the day seemed to well up in Nick's head as he stumbled out of the kitchen and tripped head-long over the body of the drunk Indian, Captain John. As Nick lifted himself off the floor he grabbed the Indian by his ear ornament and shook him to awaken him. Yanking harder than he intended, Nick's strength only served to rip the ornament off the still sleeping Indian's ear. Nick was further angered and upset by this engagement and stormed into the barroom just in time to overhear another Indian bragging as he showed his scalping knife to bystanders, "The nine marks are nine American scalps and this one is the scalp of old Stoner!"

Nick was not a revengeful person in most instances,

but for the only time in his life, he was determined to gain Old Testament justice, "An eye for an eye, and a tooth for a tooth." He knew that his father's murderer would never leave that place alive. The anger which filled his heart and mind completely overcame any reason or thought or logic that he might normally experience.

As the Indian danced around in glee, Nick grabbed the red hot wrought andiron from the fireplace and blurted out behind his hot tears of anger as he hurled the missile at the head of the warrior, "You'll never scalp another one."

Nick's hand was burned to a blister, although in his anger, he didn't notice it. He did realize, however, that the hot iron had hit the Indian on the neck and he was flat on the floor, apparently gasping his last breath.

Nick picked up a silver object from the floor near the prone Indian as some of his friends hurried him out before he got into more trouble. But the revengeful Indians, who had had enough of Nicholas Stoner, were quickly leaving with their wounded or possibly dead friend. It was lucky for them that they did because Nick's anger became more intense when he realized that the silver object was from the old head wound of his father, thereby verifying without doubt that this was the Indian who had done the evil deed.

An unnamed do-gooder seized the opportunity to "get Nick" for some past misdeed and immediately lodged a complaint with Sheriff John Littel against Nick, loudly proclaiming that it was his duty as a good citizen to protect the community against the Indians' vengeance by arresting Nick. He also piously pointed out that Nick's job as deputy didn't make him immune to justice.

Nick was promptly and willingly led off to the Johnstown jail, where a large crowd began to assemble. It wasn't long before some of Nick's Revolutionary comrades stove in the door and released Nick from jail. Nick protested loudly, but his popularity overwhelmed his objections, and he marched off to Throop's Tavern with the group.

After the group calmed down and began to drift apart, the jailer walked in and quietly asked Nick if he was ready to return. Nick good naturedly answered, "I am, if my friends will allow it," and quietly followed the jailer down the street. However, the remaining crew members again "rescued" Nick and sent the jailer home with an announcement that Nick was a law-abiding citizen and they would not see him in jail again. They also pointed out that the "dead" Indian was nowhere to be found. The jailer realized that it was useless to hold Nick now that the "evidence" had left town so he sent him on his way.

The realization of what he had done reached the conscious portion of Nick's mind as he slowly paced his way home. He had killed a man. He had snuffed out the life of one who would be missed by someone, somewhere. Nick tried to erase any thoughts of remorse or sympathy by reminding himself that his father was taken from him by the Indian. But, no matter how he tried, the dark thoughts of what his anger and revenge had caused remained with him for many years. He carried the small piece of silver as a pocket piece from that time on, squeezing it in his hand whenever he felt the clouds of anger blinding his thought and reason.

PART V

NICHOLAS STONER
Trapper and Hunter

CHAPTER XX

Nick - Trapper and Hunter

"Nick could kindle a fire — climb a tree — cook a dinner — shoot a deer — hook a trout — or scent an animal quicker than any other man."[2]

Nick liked his bucolic home in Scotch Bush, two miles west of Gloversville, the doorway to the wilderness of northeastern New York State. His nearest neighbor was over a mile away, but neighbors made Nick nervous anyway. Nick needed room, room for privacy, room for farming, and room for just getting away. And get away he did. Each year, near the latter part of September and sometimes in the spring, Nick would disappear into the woods for two months of hunting and fishing and trapping with or without a partner. Nick was sociable but also needed the independence gained from being by one's self.

Nick was always well-prepared for his forest journeys and ofttimes his wife Anna wondered how he did it. But years of practice and learning to live with hardship had built determination and drive in Nick that were unequaled in his day. Nick always jokingly said that "if you enjoy it, it can't be called work."

Nick was particular about the tools of his trade. He used heavy steel traps with two springs for beaver and otter and a single spring for muskrat. He also used a forty-pound bear trap, four feet long, with two springs, spiked teeth underneath and a five-foot chain to fasten to a tree with grappling hooks. Nick had trapped at least ten bear with this monster.

---

[2] Jeptha Simms TRAPPERS OF NEW YORK.

State of New York }
Fulton County } On this 13th day of March 1853 personally appeared before the County Court of the County of Fulton and State of New York Hannah Stoner a resident of the Town of Johnstown in the County of Fulton and State of New York aged fifty two years who — being first duly sworn according to law, doth on her oath make the following declaration in order to obtain the benefits of the provisions made by the Act of Congress passed on the 3rd February 1853 Granting pensions to Widows of persons who served during the Revolutionary war; That she is the widow of Nicholas Stoner deceased Who was a private & Fifer in the army of the Revolution; That he said Nicholas Stoner on account of his said Services was awarded a pension under the act of Congress passed 18th March 1818 at the rate of Ninety Six dollars per annum; That his services were rendered in the New York State Line in said army, which fact and other particulars regarding said services are set forth in his papers on file as declarant has been informed and believes in the matter of his application for a pension under said Act of 18th March 1818

She further declares that she was married to said Nicholas Stoner on the twenty Second day of April one thousand Eight Hundred and forty At Johnstown by James I Feldtroth Esqr a Justice of the of the town of Johnstown Fulton County & State of New York and has moved off to the State of Wisconsin, That her said Husband died on the twenty fourth day of November one thousand Eight Hundred & fifty three, that she was the widow of Henry Frank deceased before She was married to the aforesaid Nicholas Stoner, That she was not married to him prior to the second day of January Eighteen Hundred but at the time Stated above; She further declares that she Hannah Stoner is now his widow and still unmarried

Sworn to and Subscribed   Hannah X Stoner
before me 13th day of March   mark
1854.   N J Johnson
                    County Judge of
                    Fulton County

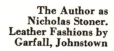

Original Grave Marker
Kingsborough Cemetery
Property Johnstown Historical Society

The Author as
Nicholas Stoner.
Leather Fashions by
Garfall, Johnstown

New York Roll.

(No. 1695.)

Nicholas Stoner,
Private
New York line — 1777. 6 years
in the army of the United States during the Revolutionary War

inscribed on the Roll of New York
at the rate of 8 Dollars per month, to commence on
the 8th of April 1818.

certificate of Pension issued the 30th of June 1818
and sent to the Pensioner at
Johnstown, New York.

arrears to 4th of Septr. 1818.

4 months 27/30. $ 39.20

{ Revolutionary claim, }
{ Act 18th March, 1818. }

Van cortlandt

Town Unknown } Montgomery

Warrant No. 12.893

160 acres
WAR OF 1812.

Act of 24 Dec 1811 9 any 11 1812

Warrantee Nicholas Stoner

Soldier Nicholas Stoner
Fife Major

Service 29th Inf

Nature of claim Bounty Land
Single

Some pots & Kettles Value ~ ~ ~ ~ 7.—

Some tea cups & Crockery ~ ~ 0.50

13 Traps for Hunting ~ ~ ~ 9.75

1 plough ~ ~ ~ ~ ~ ~ 3.25

1 chain Iron ~ ~ ~ ~ 2.

$ 91.00

And that he the said Nicholas is indebted
for the Above and Other articles to an amount
exceeding the above Sum of 91 dollars

Deduct 5 Dollars in the favor of the man
leaves the whole Amot of personal property at
the sum of 86 Dollars

N Stover

State of New York
Mont: C: Clerks Office

I John McCarthy Clerk of
the Court of common pleas in and for
the said County do hereby Certify
that the foregoing Oath and
schedule thereto annexed are truly
copied from the Records of the said Court and I
further Certify that it is proved to the satisfaction
of the Court by the Oaths of Creditable witnesses
and that it is the Oppinion of the said Court
that the total amount in Value of the property exhibit-
ed in the aforesaid schedule is $ 86. in Testimony
whereof I have hereunto set my hand and affix
ed the Seal of the said Court On the 15th day of June
1820: John McCarthy Clerk

By His Excellency

GEORGE WASHINGTON, Esq;

General and Commander in Chief of the Forces of the
United State of America.

THESE are to CERTIFY that the bearer hereof *Nicholas Stone, Fifer* in the *Second New York* Regiment, having faithfully served the United States *Six Years* nd being inlisted for the War only, is hereby DISCHARGED from the American Army.

GIVEN at HEAD-QUARTERS the

G Washington

By His EXCELLENCY's
Command,

Trumbull Jund Secy

REGISTERED in the Books
of the Regiment, *Chris Muller* Adjutan

THE above *Nicholas Stone* has been honored with the BADGE of MERIT for *Six Years* Years faithful Service.

29 acres of land as tenant at will Personal estate One mare One cow three hogs two calves some fowls one chest of drawers &c, some 4 pots and kettles half dozen knives and forks half Doz. tea cups and saucers, other things for cooking thirteen Hunting Traps One gun One Iron chain His family consists of four persons his wife Anna aged about fifty seven years in infirm health his son Obadiah aged nineteen years his daughter Catharine aged eighteen years That he is by occupation a Farmer & day Laborer

N Stone

Sworn to and declared on the
15th day of June 1820 in
Open Court   from County Clerk

Schedule of property real and personal now owned and belonging to Nicholas Stone dated this fifteenth day of June 1820 to wit

Real estate now occupies a lot of land as tenant at will

Personal estate

One mare — — — — — — — — — — — — — —	$40 —
One cow — — — — — — — — — — — — —	12
3 Hogs — — — — — — — $1½	4.30
1 Calf — — — — — — — — — — —	5 — —
Some fowls — — — — — — — — — —	1 —
some old knife & forks abot ½ Dozn — — — —	1 —
1 chest of drawers old — — — — — —	5

HEAD-QUARTERS, June *Eight* 1783.

THE within CERTIFICATE shall not avail the
Bearer as a Discharge; until the Ratification of the definitive
Treaty of Peace; previous to which Time, and until Proclama-
tion thereof shall be made, He is to be considered as being on
Furlough.

GEORGE WASHINGTON.

By order of Lt. Col. N. TOWSON, commanding the Champlain Department.

TO ALL WHOM IT MAY CONCERN.

KNOW YE, That *Nicholas Stoner* a *Fife* ~~Captain~~ *Major* of
~~captain~~ *twentyninth* regiment of *Infantry* who was enlisted the *thirtieth*
day of *March* — eighteen hundred and *fourteen* to serve during the war, is
hereby honorably discharged from the army of the United States, having faithfully
served out the full period of his enlistment.

Said *Nicholas Stoner* was born in the *City of New York*
in the *State* of *New York*, is about *fortyfive* years of
age, *five* feet *Eleven* inches high, *light* complexion, *blue* eyes,
brown hair, and by occupation, when enlisted, a *Farmer*.
Given at the Inspector General's office, Plattsburgh,
this *29th* day of *June* 1815.

S. Churchill
Adj & Insp Gen & I Gen
Genuine G. Bender Capt 29 I

Nicholas Stoner Monument
Caroga Lake, N. Y.

Nick counted his rifle almost as a friend. It not only protected and fed him but helped him to earn a living. His rifle was similar to one owned by his sometimes partner, Nat Foster. It had a single barrel with two locks, one set so that the upper charge of powder rested upon the lower bullet. The locks were made for percussion pills. It had cost Nick over $70.00 on a special trip to Salisbury to see William Avery. Nick knew right away when he saw it that it was the rifle for him, and he immediately carved his name *N. Stoner* in the stock so there would never be a mistake as to who was the owner.

Nick also filled his pack basket with a good supply of ammunition, a jug of rum, his flint and steel and tinder, and a carefully prepared supply of food. He carried a hatchet and knife in his belt and a compass in his pocket. Many times, he also added his bear-paw snowshoes for the wet woodland snow to the load.

Nick's dog, "Meeko," was a constant companion when his master was traveling alone. The friendship between man and beast was never more evident than that which existed with these two who shared many a trial and trouble in the wilderness. Nick also had a faithful pack horse which sometimes accompanied him as far as his hidden canoe.

Anna could always tell when Nick was planning a journey into the wilderness. In he would come with an old black pot, build a slow fire in the fireplace, and begin to simmer his magic ingredients — pine tar, castor oil, and pennyroyal oil in a 3:2:1 mixture. When this smelly ordeal was over and bottled, later to be rubbed on any exposed portion of one's body, Nick would guarantee protection against any wilderness "skeeter" and Anna then knew he was ready to go.

Nick was a scientific hunter. He always knew what

he was after and studied it carefully. Nick planned to shoot at least one moose per year partly for the meat and partly to prove to himself that he was still able to call and stalk such a wary and dangerous adversary. Nick had studied the moose, again following his rule that a hunter should know as much about what he was hunting as he could possibly learn, and had found that certain calls, used at the right time, always resulted in attracting a likely candidate for his rifle ball. Many disagreed with Nick's methods of moose hunting but had to admit that he always got results.

Nick had fashioned a horn of black birch about eighteen inches long. The mouthpiece was the size of his thumb, and the other end was about five inches in diameter. Nick insisted on using his own horn and, over the years, gained great confidence and skill in its use.

Nick liked to wait until fall to do his "calling," when the foliage was off and the game had begun to travel into the water. Nick found his most successful calling after the first frosts. He also liked to be up and at it in the early dawn. He usually stationed himself near a small pond knowing that if the moose is not in the water he is napping close by.

Nick attached great importance to the type of call that he used. He never gave a long, loud call used by inexperienced hunters who simply succeeded in scaring the wary moose away. Nick had learned that no note should be held but should rise and fall and end sharply. He sometimes used a combination of two short grunts of the bull moose followed by a sort of long call of an old cow. Nick, in his usual logical fashion, explained that a bull moose in the open would be challenged by the first two, and especially so if he thought a cow was around. Nick sometimes began his special call before daylight in order to give the moose enough time to get within range. He had called them from as far away as three or four miles when the wind was right.

Nick was also a good listener. He usually spaced his calls twenty minutes apart and spent the intervals listening. Good judgment played an important part in listening and responding to the answering moose. Many said that Nicholas Stoner had the gift of careful listening. He knew how to respond and was never guilty of scaring his prey away. He had even been known to wrap his horn in his coat and fool an approaching moose into thinking that he was much farther away. Again, Nick knew his opponent and used every trick in the book to outwit him and thus return home from a successful hunt.

Nick also enjoyed hunting the wild turkey of the climax forest. He liked nothing better than to return home with a turkey for the table. His family liked the tender white meat much better than some of the tough bear or moose steak that their father enjoyed so much. The wary hunter also had a few tricks to fool the turkey. Secreting himself behind a fallen log, with his rifle ready, Nick would slyly rub two pieces of cedar together, thus imitating the voice of the turkey. He also had another method developed during the winter months around the fireplace. It consisted of a cedar stick with a corn cob on one end. Rubbing the opposite end on a piece of slate resulted in a call unresistable to the wild birds. Nick also could make a turkey noise by blowing on a turkey wing bone but told his companion that it was unfair to catch a bird using one of his relatives for a lure.

Nick was noted for his ability in outwitting forest game. It was also well-known that Nick never trapped or shot any of the forest creatures unless he needed them to feed his family or supplement his farm income.

Those who committed the crimes of the woods — catching bushels of fish or simply shooting game for pleasure—avoided the notorious Nick, who could deliver a lengthy dissertation on the importance of preserving the inhabitants of the wild.

Chapter XXI

Nick and Might Makes Right

It takes a special breed of man, hardy and courageous to leave the comfort and security of a good home
to venture forth into the great wilderness. Nick's wife
often wondered and worried about why he began his
yearly preparations well in advance and, when the day
came, either ventured forth alone, with one of his fellow
trappers, or to meet an Indian friend. She knew it wasn't
the money, although he usually had a successful season.
She also knew that Nick himself could give no reason
for his annual foray into the wilderness. The intangible,
unexpressible, unquenchable, irrepressible urge to penetrate into the vast unknown territory in Nick's back
yard was much the same urge that had driven man in his
quest into the unknown since the dawn of mankind. And
Anna knew that Nick, much as his Indian friends,
claimed ownership of the vast wilderness territory included in his ventures.

Nick approached a wilderness journey with uncontrollable anticipation but always with a tinge of fear. He
knew that the wilderness could claim him at any time,
and he often mentioned that he could think of no better
way to enter the next world than to journey into the
forest and disappear. He often thought about the possibility of dropping into a swamp hole or over a hidden
ledge; he thought of ending up a loser with one of the
wild creatures — he had often spent the night near his
fire with a huge black bear hovering over the blinking
rim of light, and he had often heard the wolves in the
night as they picked up the man-scent and circled in to

investigate — and he often thought that some accident would keep him from making his way out of the mountains — yet, the urge to go far outweighed his trepidations, and he filled his pack again and again for his venture into a wilderness adventure.

Nick and his good friend, Jim Dunn, had established their camp on the banks of the Sacondaga River. Upon their arrival they had immediately set their traps. Since this was to be their home for about a month, they constructed a couple of small huts of elm tree bark. However, in their more permanent hunting, fishing, and trapping country, they erected lean-tos. Nick had spent many years working on and planning the best shelter for the mountainous summer and fall climate — warm days and cool nights. He needed a shelter large enough to hold his supplies and any companions who might join him — yet small enough not to be a major construction job. After trying many types of shelters — tepees, bark huts, evergreen-covered frames, caves, and even sleeping under the stars — Nick decided that a log lean-to, made of available trees, would serve his purpose best, along with a large native-rock fireplace for warmth and cooking.

Nick began his construction by selecting a large sixteen-foot log to form what he called his "deacon's" seat across the front. He liked to get one over twelve inches in diameter so that he could flatten across the top for better walking and sitting.

Nick generally used logs about nine inches in diameter for the rest of the structure, using ten-foot logs from front to back. The entire structure was made of logs on three sides with an open front and a bark, or when possible, a shingled, roof. The roof sloped from the front to back with a short overhanging roof angled down in front to keep out the wind and rain. He used the readily available moss of the forest to fill the crevices, making the finished structure air-tight on three sides. His friends used to joke about his "half-faced camps," as they called them, because they looked like someone had left about one-half of a log cabin unfinished.

Nick built lean-tos on Little Tupper Lake, Piseco Lake, and Mud Lake, usually facing the east. He loved waking up in the morning, watching the chilling mist move off the lake, and seeing the bright sun's rays break through as the sun rose above the mountain horizons. Although Nick had spent many hours quietly watching the sun begin his day, he never ceased to be spellbound by his enjoyment of such a "happening." And as he lived he never ceased in his enjoyment in sharing the scene with another, little dreaming that many would join Nicholas Stoner, as his spirit lives on, to enjoy the birth of the morning over a mountain lake.

Another immediate camping job was to begin work on a birch-bark canoe. The Indians had taught Nick their method of making these lightweight, fast, swiftwater craft. Nick began by outlining the shape of the canoe on the ground, clearing away the weeds and brush and then digging out a mold in the clay soil. The next step was to make ribs of white cedar, wet them and heat them over the fire so they would bend to the right slope. They were then fastened in the mold with a line running across the top and staked to the ground outside the mold. Sometimes he cut some long slats four to five inches wide and thin on the edges and fastened them the long way for a lining. Spruce gunwales were then readied and sewed to the ribs for the whole length on both sides, using spruce roots for lashings. The completed frame was then removed from the earth mold and covered with pieces of birch bark, wet and heated and stretched to fit the shape of the canoe. The bark was sewn together with spruce root and sealed with boiled pine pitch. Nick had gained some skill in making the birch bark canoe and would have matched his product with any made by his Indian friends.

Once the camp was fully established, the two woodsmen selected six or eight of the best newly trapped beaver pelts and set out for Chase's Patent (Bleecker) for provisions. They went part of the distance by canoe, leaving it hidden and out of the sun so that the seams wouldn't melt, at a point where the Trout Lake outlet flows into the Sacondaga. The overland distance was covered quickly with Nick in the lead and Jim stepping fast to keep up. When Nick hiked, he set his sights ahead and moved quickly and quietly until he reached his destination. Jim often thought Nick lost his sociability when he entered the woods.

Returning a few days later, the two checked their traps and found the first one missing. With a trap being the livelihood of the trapper, a missing trap, especially if taken by another, constituted a major crime. And Nick was well known for his persistence in reclaiming his traps when they were missing.

It wasn't long before they overtook, with the aid of their canoe, two St. Regis Indian trappers near Trout Lake. Nick quickly recognized his own trap over the shoulder of one of the Indians. Nick loudly began to argue over the ownership of the trap. Meanwhile, the other Indian drew his knife and was about to intercede on behalf of his friend, when Dunn, still in the canoe, raised his loaded rifle and shot him dead on the spot.

The remaining Indian, fearing for his own life, ran

off into the woods. Dunn, in his haste to pursue the fleeing Indian, jumped out of the canoe into the water up to his waist. He then attempted to fire a shot in the Indian's direction but his wet gun would not fire.

Nick never liked bullies and never considered himself one, always playing fair with those who played fair with him, but in this instance, when someone interfered with his livelihood, he was determined to maintain the upper hand.

Nick loaded his own rifle and went in search of the Indian camp. He found it nearby, abandoned, with a fire still burning in the make-shift fireplace. He found a good Canadian canoe, a trap, a spear and a scalping knife, and he quickly claimed them as his own, following the age-old rule of the forest, "Might makes right!"

Chapter XXII

Nick and the Adirondack Wood Nymph

It had been a particularly hot summer, and Nick had suffered more than usual with the heat, as he trudged about his farm chores. He felt that he was in need of a change of air and some relaxation. He was beginning to feel the age-old itch to get back into the wilderness. Nick knew that there was some sort of bond between him and the earth from whence he came, although he never could prove it. He told Anna that as soon as he finished the first hay crop, he was going to take a few days off for some fishing. He spent the next few evenings tying some new fish flies partially to convince Anna that he was really interested in getting some fish and partially to build some enthusiasm in his own heart and mind. Nick was tired — not sick — but tired — tired of the daily task of making a living — of dealing with others — of keeping his body going when his spirit wasn't with it. Nick had noted a few odd aches and pains, as well as being tired, and had decided that he was leaving his healthy, youthful years behind him. Anyway, it was a good time to go fishing.

Nick knew that the trout only liked a fly that imitated a natural insect as well as one that appeared in the right season, but he decided to concentrate his efforts on a March Brown. This particular fly is eagerly downed by the trout near the end of March and is still in season through April and May. Nick knew this but was anxious to see if it still worked on into the summer. Nick would feel good if he could fool the wise trout.

Nick had another reason for selecting the March Brown. He had found that by putting a little oil on the hackles and body of the fly along with rubbing deer fat on his fish line, he could fish with a floating fly. He had good results with this method of fishing simply by placing the fly on the water where he thought the trout were and letting it float over their heads with the current. Nick loved to deceive the timid trout in this fashion. It was what Nick called a very flexible fly.

Nick used the chocolate-colored fur from the face of one of his rabbits to form the body. Using two strands of partridge feathers he formed the tail, and using a brown mottled feather from the partridge's back he simulated legs. The entire fly was tied with a fine brown thread rubbed with beeswax. Nick easily made several, adding them to other flies already in the collection attached to his favorite fishing hat. And now that the task was completed, Nick began to feel eager to get going and to try them out in one of his favorite mountain streams.

Early the next morning Nick was up and away, waking Anna only enough to give her a quick kiss "good-by." Nick moved easily through the early morning forest noting the hustling and bustling as the birds and small creatures of the woods began another day. The coolness of the mist-filled morning felt good to one who wanted to escape from the long, hot summer.

Nick decided to go farther north than usual, leaving his old fishing haunts behind, and find a new spot in virgin territory. He headed in the general direction of the Grass River, where he had once hunted with the Indian, Powlus. He spent the day roaming through his beloved forest gaining new strength in his body and spirit — enjoying the trip so much that he never thought of fishing until late afternoon. He decided to put it off until the next day — not being in any hurry now that he had escaped from all his worldly pressures. He prepared himself a tasty meal of hunters' stew and trail bread and washed it all down with a leisurely drink of cider-based "kill-devil" cooled in a mountain stream.

Nick prepared himself a small bed of branches and, watching the sun drop over the mountains in a final burst of red, he fell quickly asleep under his roof of stars. Nick always enjoyed watching the stars on a summer night and would probably be somewhat disappointed that he fell asleep so quickly — although a good night's sleep was what he needed the most.

The next day broke cloudy and misty with the sun breaking through only on occasion. It was one of those strange days when the mist seems to cling to the trees of the forest. Nick hiked through the high peaks not really caring about his speed and direction until he came to one of the most beautiful wooded glens he had ever encountered. The floor of the forest was covered with a soft rug of pine needles, free of coarse underbrush, with pretty pink lady-slippers sprinkled here and there. He could hear the bubbly motion of a mountain stream at the far end of the glen, but the rising mist made it impossible to see.

Nick moved cautiously forward, thinking that this might be just the fishing stream full of trout that he was looking for — although he knew that he could catch all the trout he wanted nearer home. Breaking through the mist, Nick found himself at the brink of an overhanging cliff — looking down into a clear pool at the foot of a foaming waterfall, tumbling over the mountain rock.

Nick was overwhelmed by such a breathtaking sight of nature's beauty, and he blinked his eyes with excitement.

Suddenly, Nick was startled by a movement in the pool below as something reddish brown, possibly a beaver, broke the surface of the still water. Looking again, Nick now clearly saw the body of a beautiful girl with long red hair. Her soft white body moved gracefully and smoothly around the pool as she dove and surfaced, turned and twisted through the water. Nick blinked his eyes again and again, unable to believe that such a beautiful girl could be so deep in the woods. He had never encountered such an enchanting sight in his life.

Nick watched her long enough to believe what he saw and then decided that he would be wiser to keep still and let her enjoy her privacy rather than call out, embarrass her, and scare her away. Needless to say, Nick was facing the temptation of a lifetime as he watched such a beautiful creature move rhythmically through the clear water. Nick noted that her flaming beauty and her pure white figure were as beautiful, if not more beautiful, than his Anna's — whom he always believed to be the most beautiful girl in the world.

Nick watched, as quietly as he did any of the woodland creatures, as the beautiful swimmer rose from the water and shook herself gracefully on the moss-covered bank at the edge of the glen. Nick was visibly shaken by her beautiful, soft, green eyes as she looked up and around, raising her long, red locks with her hands, shaking the clinging water drops off, as if she was searching for the sun to break through the cloudy mist surrounding the pool. A short distance away she spied a ray of sun slanting through the trees. Bounding like one of the wild deer of the forest, she gracefully pranced to the sun-lit spot and lounging on a slanting moss-covered rock, she sunned herself until she was dry.

Nick watched this whole thing with disbelief — yet knowing that it was actually happening. He rubbed his eyes and shook his head to be certain that he was awake. The movement was just enough to cause a rustle and the girl sat up, tipped her head, and listened intently. Nick again looked deep into the most beautiful, soft eyes he had ever seen, and held his breath and froze his muscles, not daring to move lest he scare away his beautiful wood nymph.

The girl waited quietly half lying and half sitting with her long red locks falling down over her pure white shoulders. She then rose quietly and stealthily moved back to the pool. Nick lost sight of her for a moment as she knelt behind some pool-side shrubs, but she quickly reappeared, pulled a loosely-fitting shaded-green gown around her statuesque body, and danced slowly off into the wooded glen.

Nick could contain himself no longer. He sprang to his feet, untied his boots, hurriedly wrestled them off, and dove headlong into the mountain pool, knowing from experience that the water is deep at the foot of a waterfall. He swam quickly across, shouting for the beautiful wood nymph to "Wait, I want to talk to you!" and charged headlong into the woods. Nick quickly realized that she was nowhere to be seen. A careful search of the area revealed no sign of a trail or even that she had been there. Nick, an experienced tracker, was unable to find a track to follow.

The frustrated Nick dropped to the soft forest floor, dripping wet, and a little ashamed and disgusted with himself, and stayed put the rest of the day, thinking things over. Nick had raised his children with the usual childhood beliefs in good fairies and St. Nicholas and little people — and now — had he seen a wood nymph and not known it, or was it a real girl camping in the area, or was it a dream — the product of too much "kill-devil"? Nick smiled sheepishly at and to himself and shrugged his shoulders resolutely.

Nick spent a couple more days in the glen — getting some sleep, and some fish, and getting his mind and body rested and cleared. He returned home in good spirits and health and tackled his daily task with new enthusiasm. Nick wisely never told anyone of his adventure with the wood nymph — and although he returned often to the deep woods, he never again found the same wooded glen; he never again saw the clear, mountain pool at the foot of the tumbling waterfall; he never again found the shaded-green, moss-covered bank; and he never again saw his soft white wood nymph with the flowing red locks and the beautiful, soft green eyes and the shaded-green gown. Nick often thought it was a good lesson — never look for something that isn't there!

CHAPTER XXIII

Nick and the Bear

Nick worked hard on his farm knowing full well that his family could not survive without the food and income it provided and that he would not be able to make his annual trip into the wilderness if he were tied to some other line of work. He liked picking his own hours to work. He also liked being close to the soil and often felt that farming was "in his blood." Nick grew attached to his animals and enjoyed their company. He also gained a sense of pride when he gazed at the long rows of ripening corn and the blowing, waving fields of wheat.

Nick had heard the stories about the "giant black bear" that had been making damaging incursions into the farmyards around Johnson Hall. Taking each story with "a grain of salt," he laughed aloud as each teller related his accuracy in shooting and bravery. Nick's experience with bear had revealed that they were usually not as big as they appeared, but he respected their ferociousness and speed when cornered or hurt, or defending their young. Nick did discover that this particular bear had been hit and wounded at least once and was therefore a more formidable foe. He left word with all who told of the bear's forays to their farms to let him know so that he might stop it before it reached the Stoner farm. Nick knew that the thought of a loose bear frightened his wife. He felt that no one should live in fear.

Nick was right. It wasn't long before he received word that bruin was in a neighboring orchard. He immediately grabbed his rifle, called Meeko, his faithful dog, and set out. Anna registered her protest, knowing full well it was futile to argue with her husband when he faced a challenge. Nick assured her that he would stay arm's length away from the deadly paws. He knew that the long claws could tear a man's arm off and that the giant jaws could do fatal damage to a man's body.

Nick quickly found the ravaging bear which, fearing the noisy Meeko, sought refuge in a tree. Nick took a quick shot as the bear scampered, inflicting only a slight wound, but slowing the bear down just enough for Meeko to sink his teeth in the bear's leg. The infuriated bear turned on Meeko and managed to grab one of his hind legs in his teeth. Luckily the leg was small or the huge jaws would have snapped it off. As it was, they simply clamped it fast so the poor dog was trapped.

As fate would have it, Nick's usually speedy reloading was slowed down by his accidentally breaking off his powder horn stopper. However, once reloaded, he charged his ferocious foe, thrust the magazine of his rifle into the bear's throat and fired, releasing his suffering dog and ending the career of the marauder.

Nick became a local hero for a few days, having ended the terror which hung like a cloud over the remote farms, and he graciously accepted the thanks and praises of his neighbors. Nick, bypassing his usual humility, said that everyone needed to feel important once in a while, and it raised his spirits to help his neighbors.

PART VI

NICHOLAS STONER
Another War

CHAPTER XXIV

Nick - Can You Keep Your Head?

Nick could not understand it. Suddenly he was without friends. The stories had been planted and stretched and circulated until it was hard to believe. But believe it they did. Friends whom Nick considered true friends suddenly believed the worst about him. How could it be? Didn't they know that he was as true and honest and as desirous of doing what he considered right as he ever had been? And why were they blaming him? Nick tried not to get upset, but he suddenly felt very tired and very alone.

The smuggling had been traced to the Tryon County area, and Nick, being the most renowned woodsman of the time, was the logical person to blame. Goods were being smuggled from Canada down through the Great North Woods. Of course, Nick had some idea of who was guilty. He suspected Cornelius Herring and Amaziah Rust. Everybody in Johnstown knew them as well as Nick did. It was also well-known that these two doubled in shady deals and probably now were engaged in the contraband trade of smuggling goods from Canada.

Nick readily admitted that he had seen goods being transported through the wilderness on many occasions, but those transporting them and their destination were unknown to him. He even remembered, on one occasion, questioning a group of Indian squaws whom he found waiting at a secluded spot in the wilderness for some unknown trader to pick up their goods. He was, however, unable to get any information from them and, as a good woodsman, he decided to tend to his own affairs.

Nick had been in the forest for over two months and was quite ragged and unshaven on his return. It was easy to see the reason strangers would believe any story about him. But Nick could not understand why those in Johnstown could take the false rumor so seriously. He determined, in his usual independent fashion, to end the rumors and clear his name.

Nick stopped off at home to spend a short time with his anxious family and learned from his wife that trouble was again brewing with Great Britain. Nick had heard the same sad news from a Canadian Caughnawaga Indian who he met in the wilderness with his daughter.

They also met some soldiers on the trail to Canada and decided that something was up. They now knew why Mason, Nick's hunting companion, had been suspected of being a spy while they purchased supplies at a stop-over in Norway. Luckily, some of the local veterans recognized Nick from the last war and the jailing of Mason was averted. Anyway, Nick could understand why the tempers of his neighbors were running high. He had learned during the previous time of trouble it was easy to blame someone at the slightest hint of coincidental guilt. Bad times breed mistrust.

Nick reached Johnstown just in time to meet abruptly with a large, noisy patriotic delegation of his "friends" who were about ready to journey to his farm to settle things with the innocent Nick. Nick always believed in meeting trouble head-on and knew that if he were given a chance to talk he could try to convince his less knowledgeable friends of his innocence.

Nick was crafty, and he knew that he would need all his wits to get out of this one. He could recall seeing

others of his fellow human beings going to the gallows
— pleading their innocence. Nick spied Mr. Rust at
the center of the group, urging them on, while giving
them someone on which to concentrate their fears and
tempers.

Nick called out in a brave voice, although to face
one's fellow man without some fear and trepidation is
unknown, "Let Mr. Rust step forward and tell us that
for which I am accused!"

With that, the crowd melted somewhat under the
brave stance of one who had done many favors for them
and had been a hero on many an occasion. In fact, some
of Nick's friends lost heart in the "witch hunt" and left
the roaring crowd. Amaziah was bodily pushed to the
fore-front to face the firm stare of Nicholas Stoner.
Needless to say, he was speechless until the crowd began
to chant, "Tell 'im Rust, tell 'im Rust."

"Nick Stoner is an Indian lover, and he knows the
woods better than anyone — we know he's the smug-
gler," blurted out Rust and then quickly added, before
Nick could argue, "Get 'im, men."

Even though he was a peace-loving man, Nick har-
bored the thought that sometimes violence must be met
with violence. He quickly drew his hunting knife, still
fastened to his hip, grabbed the sly Amaziah Rust and
swung him around as a shield, shouting, "One more step
and Amaziah will be bleeding like a stuck hog." Nick
couldn't have been more clear as the group sobered up
quickly and waited for his next move.

Nick decided to gamble all on the fact that he knew
Amaziah, although a noisy bully, to be a coward. He
also assumed that his suspicions were correct and that
Amaziah was connected in some way with the smuggling. He placed the sharp part of his blade against the

right side of his captive and announced, "Amaziah has something to tell you, boys, and it will be the truth, not the rumor he has been spreading around in my absence."

Amaziah got the message, and fearing the sudden death met by Nick's pigs at slaughter time, he quickly confessed his crimes, blaming his dealings with the Indians and smugglers on the bad influence of his partner, Mr. Herring, and the lack of trade in Johnstown during the past season.

The crowd disappeared as Amaziah was rushed off to jail, and Nick's friends and neighbors assured him that they "never believed the rumor anyway" and that "he was right all the time." Nick simply felt relieved to have his name cleared and a chance to return home to his family and farm and to live in peace and harmony with his neighbors.

CHAPTER XXV

Nick and the Champlain Country

Nick was never one to start something and not finish it, and it was this sentiment that finally enabled him to convince Anna that he had to go again to the aid of his country. Anna had lost one husband to her country, and, although she never mentioned it, she feared Nick's departure more than anything else. They both knew that the war had killed Nick's brother John at Sacket's Harbor the previous winter even though the official cause was chickenpox.

The British had been antagonizing the new nation so much so that it might be said she was asking for war. John had re-enlisted shortly after the formal hostilities had begun in 1812, and Nick now felt he should join his brother. It was extremely difficult for a loyal and patriotic man like Nick to stay at home while others were protecting home and country. And, besides, his father had helped to end the war, and Nick wanted it to stay ended, once and for all.

Nick soon looked up his friend, recruiting officer Lieutenant Henry Van Antwerp, and joined the 29th New York regiment at Johnstown, serving with Colonel Melancthon Smith. Nick was immediately assigned to the company of Captain A. P. Spencer. Bidding farewell to his tearful wife, he left for Fort Stanwix. Later he went to Sacket's Harbor for the fall and to Greenbush for winter quartering. Nick had received his favorite position, chief of scouts.

Nick enjoyed the company and companionship of the camp life, but he was a man of action and was anxious to get moving. As soon as the snow stopped and the ice began to melt, the company made the hike to Whitehall. Nick had passed through Whitehall in the last war and noted many familiar sights along the way. The entire company moved by boat up Lake Champlain to Plattsburgh to join the army for, as Nick soon found out, some of the major engagements of the war.

Some of the Plattsburgh troops were sent to Fort Erie to secure the outpost, leaving the Champlain country in an untenable position. It wasn't long before Governor General Sir George Prevost of Canada heard about the movement of troops and made plans to attack while the time was ripe. September 3, 1814, 14,000 strong, well-equipped troops with artillery invaded the young country. Commodore Downie, in order to make the defeat complete and final, sailed a superior naval force down Lake Champlain to engage in battle with Commodore Thomas Macdonough.

General Macomb, at Plattsburgh with his 1,500 men, anticipated the invasion and sent word for volunteers from New York and Vermont to hold the enemy at bay until reinforcements could arrive. The patriotic sons of the mountains joined in numbers, many having seen service in the last war.

Men of service experience were immediately put to good use, and Nick, now a fife major, was made a field sergeant. A group of experienced marksmen were assigned to him, and many of the enemy dropped before their sights during the next eight days.

Nick had agreed with Major Woods that the least they could do was to meet the enemy north of Plattsburgh and give them a "sample" of the might of the American Army. But now that General Macomb had granted permission, and the anxious major had routed them out before daylight, he wasn't sure. They had had enough action in the last three days, and to go out looking for it took added courage. And courage they needed for they soon found out that Captain Leonard's company of artillery would not be going with them because of the lack of a direct command, the "red tape" of war.

The group, composed of two hundred men, marched out the Beekmantown Road and were joined during the early morning of the 6th by Major Appling's riflemen, who had been falling trees on the lake road to slow down the enemy, and the entire body joined with General Mooer about seven miles above Plattsburgh, just in time to hear some 4,000 of the enemy moving toward them.

The men under General Mooer's command quickly panicked and fled, causing confusion with Major Woods' infantry. The wise leader quickly ordered a charge with the words, "Shoot down the first man that attempts to run away."

Captain Van Buren ordered his men to halt and fire. Nick and his marksmen proved their skill by cutting down twenty of the enemy leaving a gap in the enemy ranks and slowing their advance. This gave Major Woods time to form his men into three groups — one in the road, one in the field and woods, and one on either side of the road. As the British advanced, the Americans could fire and retreat, passing each other as they moved and also defending each group as it moved. For a full six miles the group held off the enemy, setting an example of firmness unmatched by any others.

The late-arriving Captain Leonard and the six-pounders joined the group at the junction of the Chazy and Beekmantown Roads along with General Mooer and his militia. The British were soon unpleasantly surprised by the heavy fire but continued with overwhelming numbers, to fill the gaps in their ranks and steadily advanced. Sounding the charge, the large British force drove the courageous Americans back to Gallows Hill, their last stand on the north side of Saranac.

Nick had been too busy to think, shooting and moving with the troops, making each shot count and encouraging his men to do likewise. They had counted at least forty dead and wounded British, along with Lieutenant Colonel Willington on Culver's Hill, but their stand on Gallows Hill, even with the assistance of Major Appling, who had been summoned by Adjutant Boynton carrying a message through the enemy line, was a perilous one, and Nick was scouting around for a plan of action. Noticing the plank bridges over the rough, winding Saranac River, Nick volunteered to hold off the enemy and remove the bridge, while the troops took a stand on the south side of the river.

Major Woods liked the idea but hesitated, knowing it was certain suicide for Nick and his riflemen. The advancing enemy left little to decide, and Major Woods quickly agreed to the plan. Nick called the men together, explained the mission, told them to go with the others if they wished, which they didn't, paired them up, one man to tear off planks and the other to cover him with a rifle, and quickly began the task. The silver birches along the shore gave little cover to the brave riflemen, and Nick soon noted that his men were dropping one after another under the heavy British fire. The bridge was over half dismantled, so he ordered the remaining patriots to retreat, and breaking the few remaining planks himself, he dove into the swift-moving Saranac, just in time to escape the overwhelming barrage sent his way by the enemy.

Thus, the bravery of Nick and his marksmen enabled the Americans to hold the British on the north side of the Saranac River. Nick was pleased to hear, as he dried out over a welcomed fire, that their entire losses for the day's encounter numbered only forty-five dead or wounded. He knew that the enemy had lost well over 2,000 and his commander, Major Woods, well-deserved his promotion to lieutenant colonel. Nick had noted that the major had lost his own horse in battle and had also given one to Nick to transport a wounded soldier, William Bosworth, to Plattsburgh. As Nick held the horse while two soldiers placed Bosworth over the back, he couldn't help but admire his leader, who, in the heart of battle, would take time to help one wounded soldier.

The two armies witnessed the defeat of the superior British Navy on Lake Champlain by Commodore Macdonough in a two-hour battle on the morning of September 11th. Needless to say, the spirits of the Macomb Army were raised, and as the fleeing British headed for Canada, the Yankees fired a national salute into their camp.

Major Nicholas Stoner was again called upon to assist with a funeral procession, this time for the burial of Commodore Donnie and five British officers, and for five American officers. Nick organized a group of fifteen fifes and fifteen muffled drums and conducted the music himself. Among the selections he picked for the occasion were *Logan Water* and *Roslin Castle*. Nick picked a spot for burial among some stately pines and was known, thereafter, as a sort of caretaker and guide for both British and American visitors to the burial grounds.

By June 29, 1815, the war was over; the British gave up ideas of the conquest of America, and the American

Army was disbanded. Major Nicholas Stoner was called in by General Macomb and strongly induced to join the national army. However, he elected to take his discharge and to return to his home and family and to the wilderness he loved.

PART VII

NICHOLAS STONER
A Long Life

CHAPTER XXVI

Nick and Stump City

The clearing of land by the early settlers in the lower Couchsuchrage country appeared to be an insurmountable task. Nick was always amazed to see the rocky, timber-laden wilderness become cleared fields and farms as the settlers moved out from the population centers. He joined many a logging-bee as trees were cut and stumps pulled up; many hands made the job possible.

When Nick came back from the War of 1812 fracas in the summer of 1815, he returned to his secure and sublime life as a farmer and trapper in Scotch Bush. The clearing of land in and around Kingsborough was underway, and Nick joined his neighbors at the logging bees. It was the practice at that time to hitch a team to the stumps, using a log and chain contraption invented by the clever Nick, uproot them, and drag them to the edge of the field to form a fence of stumps. Nick gained a lot of satisfaction in seeing the sand-covered land become stripped of its large pines and a thriving little community spring up. He liked working with the New Englanders who overflowed their native area in search of farm land. He even adopted one of their rules for use in his own house, "Eat it up — wear it out — make it do!"

It had been a hot day. Nick and his neighbors were assisting Elijah Cheedle in clearing some more land for his garden and pasture. The men were facing the desperate struggle to overcome stubborn stumps, and the heat did not contribute to their dispositions as the sweat wet their clothes and clouded and stung their eyes.

Nick, always one to try to keep things on a cordial

basis, was telling stories and, in general, exercising his wit to combat the fatigue and tempers. He asked the group, "Would you believe that this land was purchased from the Indians for only three pieces of wool cloth, six pieces of garbing linen, three barrels of beer, and six gallons of rum along with a fat beast?" emphasizing each item with a rising voice and waving of arms. This action gained a laughing approval from the group so during the next lull in the activities Nick gazed around at the stump fences, now scattered around the clearing land from the Cayadutta to Kingsborough, and announced — "I hereby declare this growing metropolis to be *Stump City,* the most thriving community in the foothills of the Great Wilderness."

The men, laughing heartily, joined in announcing "Stump City! Stump City!" and thus the name uttered in jest stuck for about a dozen years.

Nick not only enjoyed the chance to hold an all-day dialogue with his friends, but he excelled at the wrestling and eating that followed a logging-bee. His early wrestling experience with his Indian opponents had made him unbeatable in a fair wrestling match, although many tried to take his "title." He also consumed more than the normal amount of food, announcing that he "lived to eat." There was no half-way with this son of the mountains. Everything he did, he did to the fullest.

Chapter XXVII

Nick the Hunter

Nick enjoyed a good venison steak or venison stew made only like his wife could make it, so when the leaves began to fall, he began to plan the hunt. Nick knew that his family needed the meat, and the hides could be put to good use, but he also enjoyed the hunt. Matching his wits and skill in the woods with the elusive deer and returning with a large noble buck filled him with a satisfaction unmatched by any of his other deeds.

Many of Nick's friends sought the chance to hunt with him, knowing full well that in this way they were assured of getting a deer. And Nick enjoyed the companionship of a good friend at a warm evening campfire. The smell of the burning wood mingling with the unmatched aroma of the evergreen forests, and the innocent scufflings and snappings of the animals in the woods filled Nick with a peace found nowhere else in the world. And having a good friend at his side to listen to his conversation while enjoying that which pleased him most, was satisfying to the devoted woodsman. Ben DeLine and Nick enjoyed many hours together in the Canada Lake-Caroga Lake country. The previous summer they had named a couple of lakes above Stoner Lake, *Stink Lakes*. Some fish had been carried over a beaver dam during a freshet and being unable to return, died when the water went down. Of course, the odor of dead fish is well-pronounced, even in the woods.

Benjamin DeLine and Jacob Frederick had urged Nick to take them to the far side of Canada Lake in search of game. Nick had found this a successful hunting spot but worried about crossing the lake with three in the canoe. However, his enjoyment of the hunt overshadowed his worries, and it wasn't long before the trio had plunged all their efforts into the hunt.

Nick practiced the art of deer hunting, and though he had no strange or secret methods, he always got his deer. Nick used to say, "My only secret is an early start —get out along the bends of the streams—and the shores of the ponds—in the marshes and along the old woods roads—and in the open sloughs bordered by thickets— find their tracks while they're still fresh. It's no job for the late riser or for one unfamiliar with the habits of our woodland creatures."

Nick knew that the deer may travel a great deal during the fall mating season but will, in general, do their wandering fairly close to their usual haunts. He had learned from experience that a buck will travel miles from his favorite range during the night but will invariably make his way back the next day. A few years of hunting and studying the ways of his prey enabled Nick to discern between an old and new track—enabled Nick to determine that a deer had frequented the vicinity.

And Nick was a quiet hunter — any noise in the woods, other than ordinary, would make the game more wary and harder to find. Nick never believed in shooting at anything except what he was hunting. A stray shot at a tree, or a squirrel or a fence or signpost was not only a waste of shot and destructive of property but was a warning to all the game within earshot.

Nick knew many other things about the deer, following the rule — to be a successful hunter you must know your game and his habits. He knew that deer feed when the moon is shining simply because at the time of the new moon they stir about later in the evening —

having stayed in their beds until dawn the previous morning, and feed well up in the forenoon. Nick knew, also, that deer are quick to adapt to circumstances, such as changing their habits when they are being hunted.

Nick knew the general vicinity of the Canada Lake area that was being used by the deer. He spent the early morning hours, as the mist rose from the sun-struck lake, showing his companions the signs of their prey and how to avoid noise — placing their heels down first along the rocky shores and stepping on their toes, letting the foot down slowly on the leaf and twig-covered forest floor.

Nick planned the middle of the day for finding the regular runways used by the deer. It was a good time to do it as it was the poorest time of the day actually to be looking for game. Nick's companions grew tired of following every path and ravine and rivulet, but their master hunter assured them that this was the only successful way to find what they sought. Nick told them to make mental notes of the feeding areas and type of food the deer were eating — these might prove handy later on when actually stalking a deer to kill.

Nick was finally satisfied that he found a good spot where the deer were likely to pass during the evening. He stationed each man against a boulder or tree where any movement would not be detected by the deer. He made certain that they had a good view of their surroundings, so as not to shoot each other, and then told them, "Be patient, and a buck will be yours before nightfall!" Being an impatient man, Ben DeLine found it hard to follow this "watch and wait" hunting method. But Nick guaranteed success, and the trio's patient planning was rewarded by the sudden appearance of two large deer. Nick allowed his companions to shoot first, using his own shot to down the larger of the two, a fourteen-pointer, after the excited Ben had wounded him.

Nick quickly used his sharp-pointed hunting knife to slit the deer back from where the ribs grow together, sever the windpipe and front and to cut around the bottom. He then pointed the animals downhill and slid their organs out. Nick liked to do the job quickly so that the hide could be removed readily and before the meat was spoiled. It was also important to get the animals off the ground before they heated up. Nick showed his friends what he called the "Garondah method." He climbed the nearest sapling, bent the top of it with his own weight, trimmed it off, slid it between the rear gambels through which a stick had been placed and, climbing off, let the tree lift the deer, with the little added help of a crotched stick.

Before nightfall, they set out across the lake for home with Nick's tree canoe barely floating with the five heavy "passengers." The water began to roll into the boat soaking the two passengers who were seated on the bottom, while Nick did the paddling. It soon became apparent that the craft would not make the journey in safety, and Nick headed it to the nearest, small, rocky island, later known as Stoner Island. The wind became worse, and the two passengers began to bail out water with their hats. Nick continued to send the boat forward with each stroke as the brave DeLine jumped overboard to lighten the load. Luckily he found bottom and proceeded to tow the boat toward shore. With this, Frederick also decided to jump overboard to make certain the saving of the game and equipment, but quickly found that he was still out over his head. Being unable to swim, he quickly sank, whereupon the gallant Stoner leaped to his rescue, grabbed him by his hair and towed him ashore.

DeLine had drawn the boat up on shore, and it was soon emptied of its cargo and water. Frederick was bemoaning the fact that he had crossed the ocean safely from Germany and now was almost drowned in a frog pond. Nick was privately bemoaning the fact that they had to spend the night on a rocky island without means of building a fire and drying their clothes — a far cry from a warm campfire in a wooded glade.

Waking during the early dawn of the chilly morning, the trio was more than overwhelmed by the beauty of the sun-filled scene before them. The now-quiet waters, surrounded by the autumn foliage, were a sight to be enjoyed again and again. In fact, the group delayed their departure as they drank in the beauty that was theirs and thanked their Keeper that they were still alive to enjoy it.

The hunters safely reached the lakeshore and got home with their deer. Frederick could not thank Nick enough for saving his life and promised that Nick would never want for anything as long as he or his children were alive — a promise which he remembered and kept as long as his rescuer lived.

Nick spent the next winter building a new craft that would be more manageable than his log canoes, yet still light enough to carry into the woods. By spring the craft was finished, and its beauty and versatility became a source of pride to its owner.

Nick wanted a boat that he could control. He wanted one that would hold one or two companions, yet light enough to carry overland. He wanted a boat which used oars for better control and mobility on the mountain lakes. Nick's experience with the dug-out had proved to him that he needed a better craft. The birch-bark canoes that he had made in the past required too much care and were hard to handle, especially when his companion was unaccustomed to paddling a canoe.

Nick decided to build his boat about ten feet long, big enough to carry a load of provisions or game, but small enough to manage over a three-mile carry. He selected clear white pine for the bottom board and the natural crooks of spruce roots for ribs. He also used knotless pine, sawed across the grain, for the siding. He put it together with screws and tacks and finished it off with a hand-carved neck yoke for carrying. It was the strongest boat for its weight that Nick had ever encountered.

Nick liked the shape and size of his boat. He showed his pride by painting it dark blue on the outside and green on the inside. His wife added to its light-weightedness by furnishing Nick with three caned seats.

Nick had seen other boats similar to his in use by some of his guide friends. He knew from their experiences it was the ideal craft for use in the wilderness. He, thereby, called this functional and beautiful craft, "My Guide Boat."

Nick hunted with many companions, the famous woodsmen, Nathaniel Foster of Salisbury and Green White of Wooster; with the woodsman Flagg, who wore a loon-skin cap with its downy coat on and with several of his Indian friends, among whom were Captain Gill and Powlus from St. Regis. Nick journeyed as far north as the headwaters of the Grass River with Powlus and learned about the St. Lawrence country from him. Nat Foster had even purchased some land back of Spy Lake on the Oxbow Tract but, knowing that this was Nick's territory, had settled in Salisbury instead.

Nick was the first, along with his Indian friend, to explore the hickory and oak timber country of the St.

Lawrence, later so important to the economy of the area. He also developed a winter trail through the frozen drowned lands of the Grass River country, saving the long trip by way of the Sacondaga River or far to the west .

At one time, camping near the head of the Grass River, the two had a visit from a French Canadian hunter and his squaw. The visitor had heard of the now famous Nicholas Stoner and questioned him about his mountain country. Nick, always willing to discuss his favorite subject, stayed up most of the night extolling the advantages of living in the foothills of the Great North Woods.

Nick was up early the next morning busily tracing a map on a piece of birch bark which would give his new friends a better picture of Stoner country. The trail, drawn by Nick, and running from Johnstown and back to the origin, later became known as the Nicholas Stoner Trail. Nick told his visitors to follow his frozen water trail or the Sacondaga trail to reach his "territory."

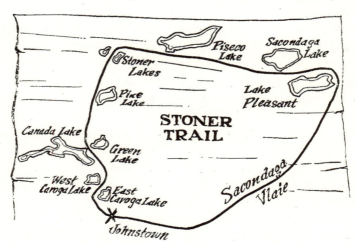

CHAPTER XXVIII

Nick and the Sugar Bush

Nick couldn't explain it—but, it happened every spring. He felt the same unquenchable urge that began in his boyhood. The approach of those warm spring days and still freezing nights signaled the time to go—time to move once again into the climax maple-filled forest, to tap her huge trees for the sweet sap, just as the Indians had taught his father in Nick's early years in the wilderness.

The cutting and splitting of the high piles of wood to boil the sap awakened and renewed Nick's muscles weakened through the winter inactivity. The gathering of the sap from each of the two or three wooden buckets attached under the hollow sumac-wood spiles protruding from each tree and carrying it to his horse-drawn barrel for transporting to his sap house filled Nick's lungs with the fresh spring air. Each step, with his favorite snowshoes underneath, holding him on the surface of the still deep but melting snow, and the even weight of the gathering buckets balanced across his shoulders with the same hand-carved yoke used so many years by his father, filled Nick with the sensation of new strength flowing through his body.

And the boys loved it. Nick's sons liked nothing better than to join their father on his spring trip to the sugar camp in the big woods. The long days in the camp watching the sap boil into syrup and into delicious maple sugar, keeping the hot fire going underneath the pan, counting the barrels of sap as they each made a gallon of syrup, helping with the gathering of the sap and carrying home the results of their some three weeks' labors to their mother combined to make "sugaring off" a never-to-be-forgotten experience.

Nick knew that it was more than enjoyment. He knew that the maple syrup and sugar would provide his family's sweetening needs for the coming year. A good season made him happy because he could share some with his friends. He also knew that this was a time for fellowship with his boys. He enjoyed their company and questions. He shared their excitement and enthusiasm as the syrup was patiently produced.

Nick enjoyed telling his sons how the Indians had shown their grandfather how to cut a small hole in the maple tree, insert one of the hand-made hollow wooden spouts and hang a bucket to catch the dripping sap.

Nick also enjoyed telling the tale of the discovery of "sweet water" by the Indians. He would call the boys together around the roaring fire, pour some boiled-down syrup on a pan of snow, and as they hastily devoured the sticky, rapidly hardening "jack-wax" with a maple twig fork, Nick would spin his tale.

"It seems that the young brave, Woranawe, was in trouble with his father, the Algonquin chief. Woranawe had used the last of his father's coveted honey. The great chief had located a great honey tree during his early years, but the wild black bear of the forest had cleaned it out the previous summer, and he was left with just a small amount to meet his needs." And, according to Nick, "the great chief loved his sweets."

Nick's children knew the importance of the honey tree and they knew how their father had placed his mark, along with the date, on many a tree to show that it was a honey tree, found and claimed by the Stoners. Nick's secret method of finding the tree by crossing the paths of two honey bees and walking to the intersection had been learned from his Indian friends. Nick had

also learned to attract the bees by placing honey on a hot fire.

"Having young Woranawe not only eat some of the chief's honey but also to devour the last of his supply heightened his anger. Handing the young Indian lad a hatchet and banishing him to the wilderness, he cried out in his Indian tongue, which loosely translated meant, 'Don't come back without something sweet to pay for your crime.'

"It was early spring and young Woranawe knew it would be a long time before he could find a honey tree, but he decided to make a camp and start his search. He quickly erected a small bark structure and set about to make a fire. His skill at making a fire by friction, using his bow, was unmatched by the other boys of his age in the village."

At this point in the story Nick would often stop, take a piece of rawhide, make a bow from a small, hardy sapling and demonstrate his own skill at starting a fire in this fashion. He always enjoyed seeing a small pile of tinder begin to smoke and burst into flame as his boys watched eagerly with childish anticipation.

And then he would go on with the tale, pouring a little more syrup on the snow to hold the listeners to the end.

"Young Woranawe started out the next day, with

his hatchet, to search for a honey tree. As he walked through the woods he began to strike the trees with his hatchet in order to find a hollow one that might serve the bees for a house.

"Returning to his camp that evening, he noticed the trees were dripping from the hatchet marks. Later on, as he lay in his bark hut, he began to dream of a woods full of honey trees, so full of honey that the sweet water would run out and supply all the Indians with the sweet goodness that his father loved so well. Some think the Great One who lives in the sky told young Woranawe about the trees; others say that he had a dream that came true; and others thought that he had been given magical power to cause the sweetness to pour from the trees of the forest. But whatever was the case, young Woranawe hurried to the trees the next morning, found them dripping steadily in the warm spring sun, tasted the liquid and found it to be as sweet as honey.

"Woranawe immediately set out for the village to tell his father the good news of the discovery. He hadn't gone far when he met his father and a group of his friends, who immediately said they were hunting, although Woranawe knew that his father's anger had cooled, and he was worried about his young son. Woranawe was proud that he had established his camp in the forest and he was even prouder when his father and the braves ran from tree to tree to taste the sweet water that he had discovered.

"Returning to the village with the news, the whole tribe began to tap the trees of the forest and to gather the sweet sap. It wasn't long before they accumulated more than they could use up, whereupon one of the squaws decided to use it for cooking instead of walking to the stream for water. It wasn't long before she found that it boiled down into an even better and sweeter syrup.

"Others joined in this venture and young Woranawe, proud of his accomplishment, began to make his share of maple syrup to pass out to his friends. However, being a boy, he soon upset his pot onto the spring snow but decided, upon seeing it harden on top of the snow, to eat it anyway."

And, according to Nick, this was how "jack-wax" was discovered from the sweet maple sap and syrup and so named today because "Woranawe" translated into the English tongue, means sugar water.

The many hours in the sugar bush were enjoyed by the Stoner "men," but they also meant hard work, and the quick end of the sap-running season was always welcomed by the tired crew. Chopping wood for the fire, gathering the sap in the snow-filled woods with a two-bucket yoke, and drawing out a sled load of maple syrup used every muscle in a boy's body, and even Nick, after many years at the task each spring, felt the results of the labor, yet, it was a satisfying job which never lost its appeal for the Stoners.

CHAPTER XXIX

Nick's Companions

One of Nick's favorite hunting partners was the Indian, Captain Gill, who was not only a successful hunter and trapper but also brought his squaw along to do the cooking. Captain Gill knew of the fear most Indians held of his renowned companion but felt the same as Nick did when it came to others stealing from his traps or hunting in his territories. However, Captain Gill, living in his wigwam at the outlet of Lake Pleasant, enjoyed sharing his territory with Nick.

Nick had learned to respect and admire the tall, stately Captain Gill both for his skill at spearing beaver in their homes and for his love and knowledge of God. Serving with the English during the Revolution had exposed the serious-minded Indian to the Catholic beliefs, and Nick noted that he continually crossed himself when danger lurked.

The two trappers, while admiring each other's skill and knowledge in the woods, were admired and envied by all those who learned of the success of the two woodsmen. Earning over $100 each from Richard Dodge at Astor's fur trading post in Johnstown for peltries taken during a single season was unheard of until the two joined forces, and their fame spread the entire length of the New York frontier. There was many a hunter and trapper who would have liked to join forces with these two nimrods who turned up many a four-pound beaver pelt.

Captain Gill enjoyed a good joke or story as much as Nick, and he delighted in telling one about his trapping friend. The Indian claimed he had heard this story among his Indian brothers, and there were those that would vouch for its truth. According to Captain Gill's account, Nick and another hunting companion, Obadiah Wilkins, were trapping in the Bleecker country, north of Johnstown, when they found themselves a little short of food. Obadiah, considering himself a better fisherman than Nick, offered to wet a line in the North Stoney Creek, a tributary of the Sacondaga, while Nick returned to camp to start a fire. Nick agreed and went off, leaving his friend sitting on a rock with his fishing tackle on his lap.

Obadiah spent a few minutes getting his line ready, only to be interrupted by a shout behind him, "What doing here?"

Turning quickly, Obadiah sizing up a tall stately, rather stocky Indian, shouted back, "Fishing!"

"Got gun?" again questioned the intruder.

"At camp," grumbled Obadiah, a little perturbed at being questioned but slightly worried over his tenuous position.

By this time, so the story goes, the Indian began to feel his advantage over the apparently helpless white man and bravely shouted, "Get out of here—Yankees no business here—this Indians' hunting ground!"

Obadiah ignored the Indian, hoping he'd go away, and the redman, having second thoughts, suddenly asked, "You got partner?"

Obadiah, seeing a possible escape to the predicament he was in, truthfully answered, "Yes, at camp, Nick Stoner."

With the sound of the famous name still on his partner's lips, the Indian was heard crashing through the woods in search of a new hunting ground. "The name of 'Nick Stoner' strikes fear in the heart of many sons of the forest," was Captain Gill's favorite line and always impressed his listeners with Nick's reputation.

Thus it was that Nick's reputation provided a protecting shield around him as he ventured into the wilderness, and this, along with his friendliness and respect for his Indian companions, gave Nick very little trouble with the original inhabitants of his beloved forest. His last difficulty with the Indians occurred at the time he shot the big moose in a pond about thirty miles in from Lake Pleasant. Nick remembered this as a sad occasion, not because of the Indian trouble, but because he always hated to kill the large and stately moose. Each time one died, his conscience felt that it might be the last of a great and noble resident of the wilderness.

Nick was doing a favor for his friend Dunning of Ox-Bow. Dunning had hidden his traps in the wilderness the previous season and was afraid to go after them alone now that he needed them again. Obadiah was with Nick at the time, but he elected to hunt with Dunning's father while Nick and Dunning went for the traps.

Nick set two of his own traps for beaver, one in a stream and the other on a small lake, and one trap for otter. It was shortly after this that Nick spied the huge moose. He quickly signaled Dunning to stop, and the two men watched breathlessly as the huge beast thrashed and jumped about in the water to fight the tiny flying pests so prevalent in the remote wetlands of the mountain. It was still a thrill to these veterans of the woods to come across one of nature's beasts in its woodland territory. Nick always said that one glimpse of a wild creature made all the walking and waiting worthwhile.

Dunning began to think that his companion was going to let such a worthy prey escape and nudged him. with his rifle giving him a questioning look at the same time. Nick knew that he would be foolish to pass up the opportunity for such a large pelt and supply of meat; whereupon, he raised his rifle just as the stately animal raised his giant head to sense his enemy. He bolted, just as the famous hunter fired, but Nick's aim was accurate as ever, and a large splash marked the end of a once-stately beast.

The two men quickly skinned the animal and sunk the hide beneath the water to get the hair off. They hung the meat in the woods along with two muskrat skins they had gotten earlier.

The completion of this task coincided with the end of a weary day, and the two decided to look for a spot to camp overnight. To their amazement, less than a half mile away they came across a bark-covered hunters' lodge and upon investigation, decided to spend the night, although it looked somewhat occupied.

Dunning was up early the next morning and upon checking the traps found the first one he came to missing. He quickly returned to the camp for Nick, who was busily baking some trail bread on a stick and preparing his morning feast. Nick knew that a good hearty breakfast would see him through the day's difficulties far better than a quick bite along the trail.

Nick soon discovered that the first trap was indeed missing although the other two, one with a beaver's leg gnawed off and the other holding an otter, were safe. He also discovered Indian trails in the vicinity and immediately knew the fate of his trap. The two hunters also heard gun shots in the distance and realized that the Indians were around. Shortly after this, on the way home with Dunning's traps, another trap was found robbed of its game and upon retrieving Nick's moose skin from the pond they found a piece had been cut off. The muskrat skins and meat also disappeared from the woods.

Nick was slow to anger and slow to speak when someone disturbed his property, but Dunning knew by Nick's fast gait and extreme silence the remainder of the trip that Nick would take some action soon. The two woodsmen arrived at Dunning's on Saturday afternoon and learned from Obadiah that two Indian trappers were at Williams' grocery store in Lake Pleasant selling furs. Nick yelled to Obadiah to "Come along and we'll fix em!" but he declined, so Dunning continued with his woodland companion, figuring he owed Nick a favor.

The two avengers found Williams alone in his store and, therefore, hastened to the inn operated by a Captain Wright. Wright told the two that the Indian hunters, Captain Benedict and Francis, had been in and were now encamped in the woods about one hundred yards away. It was nearly dark so Nick and his companion decided to stay at Wright's Inn and make a visit in the morning. During the night Wright woke Nick up to tell him that the Indians' dogs were killing his sister's sheep. Nick quickly hurried off with the nephew who had brought the news to help drive the dogs away. Nick got a good look at the dogs in the moonlight and made a mental note to tell the Indians of this misadventure also.

Nick was up at dawn and caught the Indians at their camp preparing a breakfast fire. He recognized the dogs and also noted a bushel of potatoes and some pork that the two had taken from other settlers. A bundle of traps, among which was Nick's lost trap, lay on the ground. Francis held a jug of whiskey and was busily singing a huntsman's chorus in his native tongue. Nick was recognized by Captain Benedict, who immediately told Francis who he was, as the famous hunter approached the camp. Wright, Williams, and Peck, along with a few other local residents, were also hiding in the woods watching for some action from the famous Stoner.

Nick and Benedict grunted their "hellos" whereupon the seething Nick walked forward, yanked his trap from the bundle and inquired sharply, "How did this get here?" Both Indians knew that Stoner always recogniz-ed his traps. They were made by William Mann of Johnstown who very carefully placed Nick's hun-ter's mark, his private brand, on them. Nick's early love and respect for books and learning, coupled with his intense love and respect for the great outdoors, had led him to design a brand unlike any other — a small schoolhouse sur-rounded by the outline of a maple leaf—a brand that at one glance would tell a lot about its owner.

Nick began to cut the trap loose only to be interrupt-ed by an attacking Francis shouting, "No cut him! No cut him!" The annoyed Nick swung the entire bundle and knocked the surprised Indian, who had never tangled with the wiry Nick before, flat upon the ground. This action took the fight out of the conscience-stricken Indi-an who retaliated with—"If trap yours, take him!"

Nick then proceeded to insist that the Indian hunter pay him for the stolen furs which only caused the pre-tentious and "now pious" Francis to rave and rant, much to the embarrassment of his partner Captain Bene-dict. The more sensible Captain Benedict interfered at this point and asked Nick, as an old friend, to adjourn to Wright's place of business, have a drink, and talk things over. Nick agreed to this and asked Francis to go along. The supposedly misjudged Indian did so, only after great pretense of not wanting to go with one such as Stoner.

Upon reaching the inn, Nick asked Francis to have a drink with them only to find that the insolent Indian was not about to give in and show any sign of friendship. Nick had done well to hold his temper under control for so long and, at this point, the bitter tongue of Francis was "the straw that broke the camel's back," and Nick broke the tumbler, drink and all, on the Indian's head. The Indian fell to his knees but quickly recovered and charged the angry Nick. A short scuffle followed, but Nick proved to be too much for his opponent who was thrown through the door only to land face-first in the gravel below. Regaining his feet, the enraged Indian was about to charge back in with drawn knife but was stopped by Captain Wright and other bystanders who didn't want the fight to become a deadly one. The fun was over, and the now cooling-off Indian began to pick the embedded gravel stone from his cheeks and temple.

Nick again demanded either his furs or the money and took the group over to Williams' store to prove his ownership. The Indian admitted having taken the beaver skin from the trap but denied having taken the muskrat pelts. The two made a compromise, now that their anger had been vented, and Francis paid a certain sum to settle the whole affair. Williams drew up a receipt, while the still "innocent" Indian insisted that some of the young Indian hunters were probably guilty.

And, "speaking of the devil," in walked five Indian boys, one of whom was Lige Ell, a son of Benedict, the great chief of Algonquins. Francis immediately began to accuse them of the theft, whereupon the boys wisely decided to ignore his irrational outbursts. The lad, Lige

Ell, wanted to buy a knife but found them all too light and "no more fire in 'em than there was in his nose." Nick immediately took a likin' to the boy, who had been insulted by Francis' accusations and, in an attempt to make friends with the stately youth, declaring that the moose hides, pelts, and trap proved the guilt of the older Indian, showed him his own hunting knife. The Indian boy was so delighted with it that the kind-hearted Nick told him to keep it. Once again, Nick showed the forgiveness and fairness in his heart and lack of prejudice and hatred for any man—a lack so evident in those raised in the mountains where a man is judged on his worth, not his color or belief.

On many occasions, Nick welcomed his Indian friends from the north, the Algonquins, who spent many weeks each year in the Mohawk Valley making and trading baskets for the "products" of civilization—trinkets, cloth, liquor, and tobacco. The Indian families knew that they could find lodging in the barn of the sometimes feared but always fair Nicholas Stoner.

Nick's fairness was evident in one incident occuring during a visit of some Indian families and their dog. Nick's faithful pet, Meeko, attempted to rid the Stoner home of an Indian intruder, a much smaller dog. The owner of the dog joined the fracas with a knife and tried to kill Nick's dog.

Nick was away, but his teen-aged daughter Mary called the dog into the house and slammed the door; whereupon the angry Indian stabbed the door several times with his knife. Nick arrived at this point and immediately not knowing what had preceded his arrival knocked the Indian to the ground. Two other Indians grabbed Nick just as the brave Mary handed him a heavy fire shovel for defense. Nick refused the shovel announcing that the Indians would not hurt him, they were simply helping rescue their brother. The Indians, surprised by Nick's fairness, released him and shamefully left the hospitality of his premises.

CHAPTER XXX

Nick and the Leather Industry

Nick had long realized, along with the other settlers in the foothills, that the gloves and mittens made of deerskin could be sold to others at a profit. The abundance of deer in the adjoining wilderness provided a raw material unequaled throughout the New World. And Nick, well-known for his hunting skill, determined to do something about it, thus enabling others to use and enjoy a product of his wilderness. He himself loved to wear garments made of leather.

The turn of the century had brought a lull in Nick's activity, and he had spent some time visiting friends near Kingsborough in the adjoining Stump City (which in 1828 became Gloversville.) For many years, he had been wearing buckskin mittens and breeches because of their durability and the fact that they were cheaper and easier than loom-made clothing. Visiting with the New England settlers of the area, Nick found that they were accumulating deerskins taken in trade for their tin-ware which they peddled up the Mohawk and Chenango country.

The Indians had taught Nick the tanning process using the brains of a deer which rendered a soft, pliable, durable leather. Nick sometimes substituted the brains of a hog. Nick worked hard to get the finest leather possible, spending many hours drying the skin and brains in the sun on the grass around his cabin. When he got a batch of skins ahead, he would soak them in water and take off the hair with an old knife. He generally followed this by boiling the skins and brains together in large earthenware jars in his back yard. He would wring them out and place them on racks around the yard to dry. With the assistance of his good wife, and sometimes the children, he would rub the skins continually with a stone to help in getting rid of the water and grease and to give the leather that desired soft, pliable finish. Nick often did eight to ten skins in one day. He found this method much faster than using lime to remove the hair and flesh and hemlock bark to tan the hides. The need for vats and pits and the many months of processing did not appeal to Nick's impatient nature, although he had to admit that hemlock produced a leather of excellent quality. Besides, using hemlock bark killed too many trees.

Nick made arrangements with Chester Phelps of North Kingsborough to tan some of his hides to make some mittens. This met with some modest success, and they were soon joined by Ezekiel Case of Cincinnati, who also held some knowledge of the tanning process.

Success has a way of spreading, and it wasn't long before others became interested in this venture of Nick and his friends, and many began to visit Nick to learn more about tanning and the making of mittens and gloves. Nick's process of making gloves and mittens was primitive and time consuming, consisting of cutting them out by hand using home-made shingle patterns. The outline was drawn on the leather using lead plummets which Nick made by pouring melted lead into a crack in his kitchen floor. Nick's wife did the stitching sitting on one mitten to straighten it out and make it soft and flexible while sewing the other. It soon became apparent to Nick that the venture would be too confining and monopolizing of his time. This, along with his scant knowledge of the actual manufacturing of mittens and gloves, caused him to advise two of his acquaintances, James Burr and William Mills, to seek further knowledge from one with experience. Whereupon, he recommended one of his new neighbors who had had experience in England and Massachusetts before coming to Johnstown, Mr. Talmadge Edwards. Mr. Edwards had earlier consulted Nick on the availability of the supply of deerskins in the area. Nick had become a friend of Mr. Edwards by guaranteeing an unlimited supply and also informing him that the white tail deer had coarse hair which meant a fine grained leather. The three got together, and Mr. Edwards was hired to come to Kingsborough to teach the art to Messrs Burr and Mills. By 1809, they were selling mittens up the Mohawk and soon became the first to sell them by the dozen.

Nick's reward for his initial interest in the industry was in seeing the growth of Gloversville and Johnstown into the glove and leather center of the world. Many of his friends and neighbors, Daniel Hays, William Mills, James Burr, John Ward, Philander Heacock, and Elisha Judson, to name a few, became successful in the glove industry. Nick continued to watch the wide sale of mittens and gloves and in 1825 saw Mr. Judson off to Boston with a load of gloves. In six weeks he returned with $600 in silver. And of course, Nick was guaranteed a profit from his hunting for many years to come, although he could never completely agree to killing a deer just for the skin. In fact, Nick wondered to himself, in later years, whether it had been wise to create such a demand for the skin of his deer friends.

Nick had often thought that his God worked in strange ways, and in later years, he knew that it was divine providence that saved his beloved town from extinction. Although he felt a pang of conscience each time he killed a deer, he knew that it was another contribution to the welfare of his community. The opening of the Erie Canal, a new channel for traffic and a boon to many other communities, caused a severe decline in Johnstown, which had bustled with activity as the furthermost town on the great western frontier. The stage coaches used the state road to Johnstown. Inns and taverns had grown up, only to close when the Erie took the trade away. With its colonial court house, Johnstown boasted the only brick building between Albany and the Pacific. Johnstown, once the political, social, and intellectual center for the frontier, even lost its designation as the county seat. Nick never knew how the authorities could remove a county seat from such an important historic community, the site of Johnson Hall, the site of the last battle of the Revolution, and the site which boasted the first shot of the Revolution west of the Hudson. Now real estate declined in value, wages were at a minimum, and many suffered the pangs of poverty. Nick noted that many were forced to stuff their windows with rags and crushed beaver hats to keep out the cold, unable to afford window panes. It was a community on the decline and about to die.

The developing of the glove industry during this same period actually provided the prosperity needed to support the community. Nick knew, although many would not call it such, that it was nothing short of a miracle, combined with the strength and self-reliance and industry of the early settlers that caused the growth of "leatherland," the growth of the glove and leather industry, and the eventual wealth and distinction from a wilderness once inhabited by Indians.

CHAPTER XXXI

Nick - The Unknown Woodsman

Nick will never know about the bronze tablet paying tribute to Professor Ebenezer Emmons as well as three unknown woodsmen at the summit of Mount Marcy, but he could never forget his joining with the surveying party that made the trip in August of 1837. Mount Marcy, known as Cloud Splitter or "Tahawus" by the Indians, remained unexplored while early adventurers were going as far as the Pacific Ocean.

Nick had met the party on the Old Military Road near Lake Pleasant along with Captain Gill and Peter Sabattis and had agreed to go along to help with the hunting and some of the heavy work connected with a venture of this nature. Nick's farm work had lessened during the middle of the summer, and he had left Johnstown in search of a little fishing and hunting before the harvest claimed his time. He had filled his pack in Lake Pleasant at Williams' store, joined two of his favorite Indian companions, and set out for one of the trout-filled mountain lakes he had discovered in his early years. In spite of his age, Nick retained his earlier stamina and skill in the woods. It might also be noted that in previous journeys in the mountains Nick, as well as his two partners, had roamed the "Tahawus" peaks in search of game and adventure. He was a welcome addition to the group.

The commission, appointed by Governor William Marcy to make a geological survey, included Professor Ebenezer Emmons of Williams; James Hall, state geologist; Professor John Torrey, botanist; Professor C. Redfield, engineer and meteorologist; C. C. Ingham, artist; along with E. Emmons, Jr.; Archibald MacIntyre and David Henderson, explorers and owners of land in the region. Harry Holt and John Cheney had been employed as guides. Earlier, the party had also secured the services of Lewis Elijah, son of the Abnaki Indian, Sabael, to guide them by way of Lake Pleasant and on to Indian Lake, across the Cedar River to Blue Mountain Lake.

It was during the trip from Blue Mountain Lake to Marcy that Nick, while hunting game to feed the always-hungry outdoorsmen, ran into a party of one of the Algonquin Indian groups. He correctly assumed they were remnants of a once proud Indian tribe now relegated to making a meager living on the reservations north of the great wilderness. He quickly noted the familiar trappings of the Algonquins and proceeded to greet them in their own tongue. Nick learned that they were travelling far from home in search of game. He recalled stories of the Algonquin aversion to farming in the earlier years and their nickname "Haderondacks" or barkeaters, from *hades* meaning they eat and *garondah* meaning trees. The Iroquois had blessed the Algonquin with the term when the hunting was poor, and they were forced to eat buds and bark. Professor Emmons, when told of the chance meeting and the old story of the "haderondacks" by Nick, laughed excitedly and announced his search for a name for the Great Wilderness was ended. He would call the wild Northern Woods, this great Couchsuchrage—the Adirondacks—in honor of the first proud sons of the mountains—the Algonquin hunters.

Nick had spent many hours of solitude climbing and exploring the magnificent sky-piercer, "Tahawus". He had trapped in the vicinity with his Indian companions on many occasions during his long career as a woodsman, and he had always enjoyed exploring the high peak region and the view of his beloved mountains from the top of his world. Nick was also looking forward to this opportunity to travel with such a fine group on an expedition to the top of the "high peak of Essex" as Professor Emmons called it.

The group headed northeast from Blue Mountain Lake and in two days reached Lake Sanford without incident. From there they moved on to the settlement at McIntyre to spend the night.

It was August 3rd when the group left McIntyre and with the help of five woodsmen was able to reach the old camp at Lake Colden by five o'clock in the afternoon, thus allowing time to prepare a hearty meal and their quarters for the night.

And such a meal they had! No one would believe the fare put forth by the experienced guides while on the trail. The group enjoyed fresh venison and trout, seasoned with sweet salt pork throughout their journey, and beaver roasted over the fire on a spit of wood, served on the inner side of clean bark. And Nick's trail bread and venison stew earned him the title of wilderness chef!

Nick and the others spent the early evening around the campfire trying to outdo each other in telling of their many exploits and experiences in the wilderness. Nick managed to get a word in with the others and warned the group to be prepared for an unforgettable evening on Lake Colden. He knew it was too difficult for him to put into words, so he told them to wait for a hand from the Unseen Power. Suddenly, the moon appeared and rose steadily over the shimmering waters throwing the shadows of Mounts McIntyre and McMartin in the background. The group was speechless. In the silence each man was alert to the many sensations caused by such a sight. Nick knew from their reactions that they each would long remember the moonlight over this mountain lake. Following a long solemn look at the evening scene, much as leaving an impressive church service, the intruders into nature's hidden beauty murmured brief "good nights" and retired quietly to their beds of spruce.

The expedition was up and away early the next morning setting Lake Avalanche as their goal for the night. Although it made their trip longer, they wanted to see the lake. The actual distance in miles was short, but the going was rough. The party knew that the sheer, steep bank of Mount McIntyre plunged directly into the water. Therefore, after a brief discussion, it was decided to forge a trail along the side of Mt. McMartin. They soon found that the trip was as rough as they expected. The fallen trees and thick brush slowed the group considerably and forced many detours, eventually causing them to go farther up the mountainside to follow some of the existing animal trails.

Nick did his share of trail breaking, and at one point, dropping through the brittle moss into some ancient, unknown lake, saved himself by his quick thinking in grabbing a near-by branch. Many of the Adirondack bogs are bottomless lakes, left by the ancient glaciers.

By the time the group reached the ridge at Lake Avalanche they were bruised and aching from their stumbles through the thicket and over fallen logs and roots. Ankles were sore from the sharp, overgrown, hidden rocks. However, aches and pains were quickly forgotten as the group sat on the moss-covered rocks and viewed the crystal clear, yet deep black, mountain lake gleaming in the afternoon sun.

The next morning Nick led the group across the outlet, where Lake Avalanche flowed toward Lake Colden and pointed out to the group how the two lakes were originally one body of water. Professor Emmons envisioned the ridge separating the two as a product of a large, pre-historic avalanche.

The group evaluated the journey ahead and decided that it would be easier to retrace their steps of the previous day, much easier now, because of the trail made by the group of thirteen hikers on the previous day. Reaching the outlet of Lake Colden, they crossed a fallen log on the head waters of the Hudson River. They immediately climbed upward, keeping the river channel on their left.

The group climbed for about a mile, keeping away from the thick riverside growth, when they heard the loud roar of rushing water. Hurrying to the river bank, they were rendered breathless by the sight of a flume charging through the passage of rock, ripping and tearing over the pointed and trapped rocks and logs. The many pools of bubbling water tempted the fishermen in the party, so they pitched camp and enjoyed a trout supper. Nick, always one to rise early while the day is young and the woods are still misty and cool, suggested an early start in order that the group could camp on the summit of the high peak before dark.

It was a tough hike, over the roughest of the Adirondack country, the many small valleys and ridges numerous logs, roots, and rocks, and the jungle-like growth of underbrush. The group paused at the occasional mountain springs for a cool drink and a rest but otherwise followed the steady hiking pace set by Nick. It was mid-afternoon when the group began to leave the river and start the steep climb through the dense wilderness of unexplored country. Soon they began the real ascent of the journey, pulling themselves almost straight up by trees and boughs, and using rocks and crevices for footholds.

The expedition began to feel the excitement of reaching their goal, noting the view of Mount McMartin behind them and the change in the woodland growth. The intertwining dwarfish pines and spruces got smaller and smaller, and the rock underneath began to show more and more. A chill began to fill the air. The steady wind began to blow. The going seemed endless to the anxious group, yet it wasn't long before Nick dropped on a mass of rock and turned to enjoy the view from the top of the Adirondacks. He was silent and breathless as always, murmuring quietly to himself as he had done so often in the past, "Thank you God, for such a wonderful world."

Chapter XXXII

Nick's Philosophy

Nick lazy?—Many said he was—how could a lazy trapper do an honest day's work—how could one who had so few possessions be considered ambitious—how could one who always moved away from the centers of population pursue steady employment? Only Nick could supply the answer — the never-ending answer reaching culmination after years of reading and studying his Bible, after years of watching his children grow, after years of placing faith in mankind, after years of sorrow and sacrifice and searching, and after years of solitude in the Adirondack wilderness.

To truly know a man like Nicholas Stoner—a man so simple in his ways—yet so complex in his thinking—thinking that throughout his life served to make him a man so fair that he held a special place in the minds of his friends and a man so wise in family ways that his wife and children were the only reasons for his continued existence on earth—was to be attuned to the ways and thoughts of one unique in history.

Nick was married to Anna for forty years. They had six children — and when Nick fished, the six children fished—when Nick hunted, the four boys joined him as soon as they could carry a rifle — when Nick put in the long hours to prepare the ground, plant and care for the garden, and to harvest the crop, the family was with him. Nick knew that he could sacrifice his family for higher wages and more secure work. The sheriff's job was his for the asking shortly after his term as deputy—but he walked away from it—knowing full well that a job serving the public would require all his waking hours and devotion—hours that could be spent with his children and devotion that could be spent on his family. And Nick was wise enough to know that the time spent with his children would, in the long run, make the job of the public servant much easier.

Those who knew Nick admired his family devotion and the many things that he did for and with his family. Many felt guilty for not doing the same—especially taking the many journeys into his mountains. The children joined Nick, as he penetrated the wilderness, from the time they could hold their heads up in a pack basket. And they shared their father's love for the quiet brooks, the majestic cliffs, the cold, clear lakes, and the forest glades and glens of the Adirondacks. Nick tried to impress on their innocent minds that everything came from nature and the important things in life were free—gaining strength by leaving the stress and strain of everyday living to find peace and contentment, even if brief, in the wilderness—gaining peace of mind and heart by living in peace with his fellow man—living each day as if it were precious and as if each minute could be used for some good and not wasted on unnecessary bickering or arguing or quarreling or fault finding or complaining or promoting prejudices or bigotry. Yes—Nick worked hard at the business of living—much harder than most work at a job.

And Nick's interests varied—varied as much as the seasons—and ranged from one extreme to another— a love of the great outdoors and a love of a good book at the fireside—a love of the freedom of independent action and a love of education and the peace brought by adherence to law and order—a love of solitude and a love of the fellowship of friends and family—a love of the hunt and a love for the reverence of life. Nick never approved of killing for fun—he only believed in taking what was needed to feed and clothe his family and to make a living. It was this very dependence upon animals that created Nick's love and feelings for all of God's creatures. Nick was truly a man of many contradictions.

And Nicholas Stoner loved life. His wrinkled features revealed the happiness and enjoyment that his variety of experiences and his outlook on life brought to him. He served the community well. His years as trustee in Bleecker's school district number 4 showed his respect and belief in education. His years as a constable emphasized his interest in law and order. His service as highway commissioner and assessor indicated his interest in the growth of his community. And whatever job he did, he did to its fullest, and he always did aggressively what he thought was right whether others approved or not.

Nick had no secret for happiness other than that he actively worked at it—worked at the business of life. He was able to meet misfortune as it came—wounded in the war—loss of a child—loss of his wife . . . and then get on with the business of living—with new strength to put up with what he couldn't change. Nick had a firm commitment to the type of life he led and to his work, giving him a complete source of satisfaction—another contribution to his happiness.

Nick's years in the woods had bred in him a tolerance of uncertainty—a tolerance of uncertainty born of many years of penetrating the wilderness — accepting the unknown without feeling threatened or frightened. In fact, Nick's wife once said it was this very excitement of the unknown that attracted Nick to the wilderness.

And Nick learned to appreciate the many little things of life—an appreciation born of the wilderness, through years of being overwhelmed by a tumbling mountain stream—through years of being left breathless by the view from a mountain peak—through years of gaining a peace of soul by leaving civilization. And Nick, each time he returned home from a stay in the wilderness, felt a new appreciation for his wife and family—an appreciation that was expressed in his outward burst of affection when he greeted them and his inward feeling of relief that they were all right. Nick could never express what his family meant to him and the strength that he gained from his close family ties.

Nick searched for happiness as he worked hard at the business of living and, therefore, found more happiness than many who searched for happiness by working hard at the pursuit of worldly goods. Nick was the first to admit that his greatest happiness came from the love he shared with the women in his life.

Nick firmly believed that woman was made for man, and although he loved the solitude and aloneness of the wilderness more than anything else, he could not imagine his life without a woman. He enjoyed the many hours together with his wife, Anna. Upon her death, after forty years of marriage, he was filled with a loneliness unlike any he had ever experienced. Waking up in an empty bed, sitting alone at mealtime, and having no one to share his worldly interests made Nick a sad and desolate soul.

Nick's loneliness led him to feel a new kinship with one of his neighbors, Mrs. Polly Phye, whose husband had disappeared a few years before. He began calling on Polly if for no other reason than to have some one listen to him—Nick loved conversation and enjoyed nothing more than to talk to an admiring female. As these things usually work out—two, kind and friendly, lonely souls became interested in more than just friendship. Nick insisted that Polly marry him and move in with him immediately, but the pious Polly wouldn't hear of it until she could obtain some news of her husband's possible death. Both knew that, according to law, a wedding ceremony followed by the reappearance of her husband would place her in jail. The two, upon Nick's persuasive charm, finally agreed to a voluntary marriage without benefit of a formal ceremony. Nick again proved to be a good husband, although the two had no children. They lived together until Polly's death some twenty years later.

Nick again experienced the old loneliness but decided he was getting too old to burden some woman with his "set ways" and demanding disposition. However, as life sometimes fits into place for those who live in the right way, he met the widow Hannah Houghtailing Frank, and they were united in marriage on April 23, 1840. Although Nick was thirty years her senior, he proved to be an admiring and loving husband and she to be a faithful wife and housekeeper—taking in boarders at their Newkirk's Mills home to supplement Nick's pensions and small earnings as a guide.

Thus it was that Nicholas Stoner ended his life maintaining his daily contact with his wilderness and with the woman he loved—fulfilling a philosophy of living and loving unique to this son of the Adirondacks.

Chapter XXXIII

Nick's Final Years

Nick never could enjoy living in the center of population. Although he enjoyed good company, he once vowed he would never live with another house in his back yard. Nick liked the wilderness for his back yard and elected to spend his final years in the town of Garoga at a new settlement called Newkirk's Mills named after the enterprising Garitt Newkirk, who built a tannery and saw mill which was drawing laborers to the area. Nick's wife kept several boarders and this, along with his pension, enabled him to enjoy "a little leisure," as he called it. Leisure to Nick was getting up early and watching the chill-lined mist rise from the still water, guiding the surveyors on their forays into his lifelong domain, and talking and preaching to all who would listen about saving the wilderness which God had given to man.

"The heavens declare the glory of God; and the firmament showeth His handywork." Nick looked upon the tender shoots pushing through the hard ground; he watched the birds returning in the spring; he watched the birth of new life and the protecting mother animals; he watched the changing seasons and the rain and the snow and the sun, and he knew that they were miracles of God. Nick would ask his friends to look at a landscape or at the mountains or at the forests and think about who put them there and why they were there. And then the thoughtful Nick would ask, "Shouldn't we leave them, as they are, for our children?"

Nick enjoyed the trips into the Adirondacks with the surveyors. It gave him a chance to share his love for the mountains while making it possible for others to venture forth into his wilderness. He assisted Lawrence Vrooman in laying out a road from north of the Mohawk into Piseco country through the Ox-Bow tract. The group was large, usually numbering about twenty, giving Nick a chance to tell many tales of the Adirondacks including the now-famous story of the Adirondack Mosquito. It seems that one night the old trapper was awakened by a loud buzzing only to find a giant mosquito perched on each foot. Just as he was about to swing the butt of his trusty rifle, he heard one ask, "Shall we take him home or just eat him here?!" Nick always thought the story was good for a laugh even though the truth might be in question.

It was during this same trip that the group ran short of supplies while camped near Ox-Bow Lake, and the regular suppliers were afraid of getting lost in this strange country by going for supplies. Nick, always willing to do more than his share while camping, agreed to go through the woods to Lake Pleasant. He traveled all afternoon and arrived just at evening at the home of a pioneer family named Denny. The family knew Nick well and welcomed the opportunity to do a favor for the aging woodsman.

The Denny boys got the fireplace going, and the unselfish Mrs. Denny began to bake bread that she had previously prepared for family use and some of the neighbors. The family was busy nearly all night and, packing twelve loaves into a sack along with a large cheese, Nick took off for camp at daylight. He knew his friends would be hungry so the persistent woodsman hiked without stopping until he reached the encampment, even though the steaming hot bread was burning blisters on his back!

Nick spent many hours teaching the young men of the party, many law students, how to catch trout in the west branch of the Sacondaga. Nick had learned over the years how the trout loved the cold deep holes. He knew where the springs were hidden among the rocks and waters of the river. Nick taught his pupils that when they missed a good trout that had risen to a fly not to cast immediately in the same place. He had learned that it was best to give the trout a rest and then try again. He also encouraged the boys to try every bit of white water, for he knew that the brown trout liked it rough. Nick knew many of the little tricks important to a fisherman. He always fished upstream when fly-fishing. He had learned through experience that trout lie with their heads upstream waiting for food and insects to come floating down and when they strike they will usually head upstream giving the fisherman a better chance to hook them. Nick also learned that he didn't warn the fish of his coming by kicking up rocks and dirt ahead of him as he did on a down-stream walk.

There was no end to the little things Nick had learned to make every fishing trip a success. The surveyors always counted on Nick to come up with a new trick on each trip into the wilderness. He coated his line with deer fat so it would float for dry fly fishing. He soaked his leaders for at least twenty minutes before using them and also stained them by soaking them overnight in a solution of strong coffee. He even taught the would-be fishermen to tie strings to the things of value in their pockets in case they fell while wading a stream. Nick knew enough about fishing to guarantee a catch from his Adirondack streams every time. Yet, he still followed his life-long rule—never take more than you can use. And in this way, Nick provided many a meal for the always hungry workers.

Nick furnished another feast that the group did not soon forget. One July 3rd, Nick, crossing a mountain

ahead of the group, had startled them all with his shouting that he had found some ice between the rocks. The
ice gave Nick an idea, so, planting the American flag
that he always carried with him, where the ice was
located, he hiked to Piseco Lake to camp for the night.
Early the next morning he captured a large turtle on the
beach and from it took 172 eggs. Returning to his ice
cache, he proceeded to make chilled egg nog for the group,
the turtle meat was cooked, and the 4th of July was cele-
brated as well in the Adirondacks as it could be cele-
brated anywhere.

As Nick lived his life, so did he end it. His final years
found him roaming quietly about the woods and mountains with a dream in his mind and heart. Nick worried
about his beloved wilderness and its wild inhabitants. He
saw the endless cutting of timber — he saw the senseless
shooting of game — he saw the bushels of fish taken for
fun and self-glorification — he noted the increased number of intruders into the Adirondack wilds, and he worried, but Nick was a dreamer.

Nick dreamed with a tenseness in his heart and a
tightness in his stomach of the day when man was wise
enough and honest enough to preserve properly the
Adirondacks, as he knew them, forever. He envisioned a
forest that could give all men that peace and quiet, that
privacy and solitude, that beauty and example of God's
power that had meant so much to him throughout his
life. And he envisioned a forest that would provide all
men with the recreation that meant so much to him—
the coolness and refreshness of a swim in a wood-ringed
lake, the thrill and accomplishment of landing a lively
fish from a tumbling mountain stream, the breathless-
ness of the view from a mountain top, the increase in
appetite for campfire food, the deepness of slumber in

a cool Adirondack night, and the brief sight of wild game roaming the woods.

Nick wished that man would be satisfied to leave the woods as they found them, to be satisfied with the natural enjoyment within the confines of the Adirondacks—the abundant wild game and forest birds, the clean fish-filled mountain streams and lakes, the wooded glades and forest glens, the stately trees and hard-rocks cliffs—and not invade them with the sole thought of making money by over-cutting her trees, of over-taking her fish and game simply for pleasure, of over-filling secluded inwards with noise and crowds and confusion and, the biggest crime of all, pollution and litter, destruction and deso-lation, and thereby spoil forever a moment of silence for a lover of solitude, spoil forever a special scene for a lover of beauty, spoil forever a woodland creature or a majestic rock, a trickling, sweet-tasting stream or a wooded mountain. After all, as Nick had learned, what is money and false pleasure if man cannot find peace and enjoyment; what satisfaction does man truly find in killing any of the woodland creatures for the "sport," and what kind of men can be content with leaving a path of litter and destruction and pollution and desolation in a world once filled with shaded woods and quiet brooks and the birds of the air, the animals of the wilderness, and the creatures of the waters? Yes, Nick thought, can man truly have dominion over the wild creatures and his mountains and woods and be certain of their existence for all the generations to come? Nick promised his wil-derness to his grandchildren—that they could walk where he walked, see what he saw, do what he did, and find life on earth a little better, and Nick pictured the grandchil-dren of his grandchildren struggling in a future world, but still returning to his wilderness for the inward strength to face the outward life.

Each spring Nick would return to his favorite mountain stream and feel the strength of springtime flow, once again, much as the rushing mountain stream came off the mountain, through his body and fill him with renewed energy and spirit to face the rigors of life. And as he stood in the solitude of the rushing springtime stream, the rays of the warm spring sun angling through the trees, he would allow his wrinkled eyes to squint at his surrounding mountains and mumbling to himself as he had done so many times throughout his adventurous life, "I will lift up mine eyes unto the hills, from whence cometh my help." The aging Nick, the true son of the Adirondack Mountains, the true son of the Adirondack wilderness, would dream of the day when he would **reach the** eternal springtime, and forever be a part of the earth from whence he came.

About the Author

Donald Williams was born and raised in the Adirondacks. He was educated at Northville Central School, earned his BS at SUNY Plattsburgh, and his MS at SUNY Albany. He is a retired school administrator and a licensed Adirondack guide.

Williams has written numerous articles for magazines including *Adirondack Life* and the *Journal of Outdoor Education* and served as Adirondack regional editor of New York Sportsman for over eighteen years. He is the author of several books of Adirondack and local history.

Williams and his wife, Beverly, live in Gloversville and have five married children and several grandchildren.